George Sand

Indiana

Mauprat

Janet Hiddleston

formerly of
St. Hilda's College, Oxford

UNIVERSITY of GLASGOW
FRENCH AND GERMAN PUBLICATIONS
2000

University of Glasgow French and German Publications

Series Editors: Mark G. Ward (German)
Geoff Woollen (French)

Consultant Editors: Colin Smethurst
Kenneth Varty

Modern Languages Building, University of Glasgow,
Glasgow G12 8QL, Scotland.

First published 2000.

Printed by The Book Factory, London N7 7AH.

ISBN 0 85261 660 0

Contents

Note on editions

The Gallimard 'Folio' texts of *Indiana* (no. 1604, ed. Béatrice Didier) and *Mauprat* (no. 1311, ed. Jean-Pierre Lacassagne) are the base editions, and page references to them are given in **bold** Arabic numerals between brackets, e.g. (**94**). The same convention applies to citations from their prefaces and critical appendixes.

Excellent translations of *Indiana* and *Mauprat*, by the late Sylvia Raphael, have recently appeared in the Oxford University Press 'World's Classics' series. They both contain an introduction by leading Sand scholar Naomi Schor, and useful explanatory notes.

References to arguments rehearsed in books and articles listed in the select bibliography, or direct quotations from these, are associated with the critic's name and denoted in the text by a simple page reference. Where more than one piece of scholarship by the same person is involved, a simple numbering convention has been adopted, e.g. (*1*, p. 43).

Quotations from George Sand's *Histoire de ma vie* and *Lettres d'un voyageur* are taken from vol. II of Sand's *Œuvres autobiographiques*, ed. Georges Lubin (Paris: NRF Gallimard, 'Bibliothèque de la Pléiade', 1971). The autobiography title has at times been abbreviated to *Vie*.

It has been necessary to work from the hard copy of the late Janet Hiddleston's manuscript, and any blemishes resulting from this are not the author's. The scholarly help generously offered by James Hiddleston (Exeter College, Oxford), Sue White (Nottingham University), and Nigel Harkness (Queen's University, Belfast) is most gratefully acknowledged.

Foreword

The name of one woman stands out among the many celebrated male writers of the nineteenth century in France: George Sand, born Aurore Dupin in 1804, whose long life spanned three quarters of the century. She was considered the equal of them all, was the intimate friend of Balzac, Musset and Flaubert among others, and was admired abroad by George Eliot, Dostoevsky and Henry James. She took some part too in the political life of her time, particularly during the months after the February Revolution of 1848, when she briefly acted as unofficial Minister for Propaganda. She was nominated for membership of the Académie Française and the Assemblée Nationale, but refused both on the grounds that it was too early for the election of women to such prestigious institutions. The Saint-Simonians wished her to become their female Pope, an honour she declined (360). As a friend of Louis-Napoléon Bonaparte, Emperor of France from 1851 to 1870, she used her influence to plead for mercy on behalf of some of her former political allies. Most importantly for us, she was a prolific writer of fiction, whose novels were among the most widely read and discussed of the period.

How strange then that for almost a century after her death she was remembered only for her status of (to quote the title of a television dramatisation) 'notorious woman'. Her colourful personality was associated with public separation from her husband, conspicuous love affairs with Musset and Chopin (among others), and the caricatural image she left behind of a cigar-smoking, trouser-wearing bohemian, a stereotype which corresponded to the truth of but a very few years of her life in the 1830s. From her huge literary output, the only novels that were still read were *La Mare au diable*, *La Petite Fadette* and *François le Champi*, her three rural tales set in her native Berry, and even these were seen largely as stories for children. Interest in her revived in the early 1970s as literary critics, particularly women, realised the potential richness of many so-called minor writers, often women deemed unworthy of inclusion in the canon of great authors because they were too sentimental, too idealistic, too subjective, too long-winded: in other words not sufficiently 'male'. Sand was found guilty on all these counts, sometimes unjustly since her writings range very widely, covering social, political and philosophical as well as personal issues.

The historical and literary value of these 'women's' texts has now been recognised, and our growing familiarity with them can help us understand what it was like to be a woman in an earlier century, not only through the situations of such female protagonists as Indiana and Edmée, but also through the perspective taken on them by their creator, also a woman. It seems that women write differently from men about the world, so that our interpretations of their works should take their gender into account, just as our analyses of texts by men should contain an awareness of their social and cultural context, which includes their gender. Feminist criticism is based on just such an awareness, which, without denying the validity ot other kinds of criticism, be it Marxist, structuralist, psycho-analytical or stylistic, can stimulate readings which are completely new.

So George Sand has come back into her own, and in the last twenty-five years has inspired numerous studies, of her life, which never fails to interest, and of the full range of her works, their sources and influence. In pursuing this research, critics have generally found that her literary career appears to fall into three distinct phases. During the 1830s she wrote chiefly personal novels, concerned with intimate relationships, love and marriage, and inspired to a greater or lesser extent by her own experiences. Towards the end of the decade and after 1840, her writing became more ambitious, more politically and socially committed or more philosophical. For the last twenty years of her life, her prolific production of novels of many different kinds on various subjects continued; some of these are surprisingly original, but they fit less easily into any category as writing became more and more simply part of her routine.

As an introduction to Sand's writings, I have chosen to bring together *Indiana* (1832) and *Mauprat* (1837). As well as being works of interest and value which can be enjoyed in their own right, they are also very different, and give a clear sense of Sand's development as a writer in the first decade of her literary career. It took some time for her to find her voice. Although this is probably true of most great writers, it was particularly difficult for Sand since she was a woman venturing into what was seen at the time as largely male territory. There had, of course, been women novelists before, particularly in the eighteenth century, but they had tended to confine themselves to sentimental letter and memoir novels (with the magnificent exception of Madame de Staël, who had written social and cultural studies as well as two great novels, *Delphine* and *Corinne*). By adopting a male pseudonym, Sand made quite plain her refusal of any feminine stereotype and claimed the freedom to write as she liked: of the society and morality of her day, as well as of the sufferings of individuals trapped within them. And yet as a woman, however much disguised, she had a different angle or 'take' on such issues, a different way of writing about them, and she also felt a strong desire to use her novels to convey this personal, 'feminine' approach. So while following in the footsteps of her great male predecessors, Rousseau and Balzac, for example, she also needed to adapt these models to accommodate her woman's convictions, on marriage, adultery, education and social justice.

This is the main perspective from which I propose to study these two texts: to establish how successful their author is in creating a coherent and original whole out of such disparate aims and influences. *Indiana* is a bold experiment, a striking first novel which enthralled but also puzzled its contemporary readers by its sometimes awkward mixture of tones. By the time she wrote *Mauprat*, Sand had freed herself from the constraints of realism and chosen other, more appropriate and consistent models. She thus succeeded in imbuing every aspect of the text with her own strongly-felt moral idealism while avoiding any undue over-simplification; complexities and ambiguities remain, but are contained within the overall message rather than undermining it.

Indiana

(i) Context

Indiana exploded onto the Parisian literary scene in May 1832, creating overnight the reputation of its young author and establishing once and for all her new identity as George Sand, professional writer. These were turbulent times: in the last forty-three years, since the Revolution of 1789 had brought down the monarchy of Louis XVI, régime had succeeded régime with dizzying rapidity, each important political change bringing with it changes in mental attitudes and literary fashions. The latest of these was the July Revolution of 1830, which replaced the Bourbon royal dynasty, restored in 1815, with the so-called 'citizen' king, Louis-Philippe. He was a cousin of the last monarch—Charles X—from the collateral Orléans line, born of a father who had voted for the death of Louis XVI. Sand was to include this political and social upheaval in the background to her novel

Her own life too had been marked by disruption and strife. She had lost her father at the age of four, and after months of bitter disagreement between her mother and paternal grandmother over her care, was largely abandoned by her mother to be brought up by her grandmother and her father's old tutor at their country home, Nohant (Indre). They both treated her as a substitute for the son and pupil they had lost, but her grandmother also wished her to be a lady and so had her educated for two years at a fashionable convent in Paris. After her death in 1821, when the adolescent girl was seventeen, Aurore was given little choice by her relatives but to enter into an arranged marriage with a man much older than herself which totally failed to make her happy. As a result of these conflicting experiences, she had some difficulty in acquiring a stable sense of her own being, in particular of her identity as girl or boy, woman or man. We see this difficulty reflected in the gender uncertainties of some of her heroines.

By the time of the July Revolution, her personal life was also reaching a point of crisis, and in January 1831 she left her husband and two children at Nohant to establish herself with her lover, Jules Sandeau, in the archetypal Parisian *mansarde* overlooking the Seine and the cathedral of Notre-Dame, returning to Nohant only at three-monthly intervals to see her children. In Paris, she led the liberated life of a student, assuming men's garb to give her greater independence and anonymity. She frequented theatres and cafés, wrote features for *Le Figaro* and, in collaboration with Sandeau, tried her hand at fiction. However, it was in the quiet and solitude of one of her visits to Nohant that she wrote *Indiana* in the early months of 1832, and the novel appears as the expression of all her accumulated experiences so far: those she had lived through in her unhappy marriage and abortive love affairs, but also those she recreated in her imagination from the many books she had devoured during her lonely adolescence and early married life.

It is the first novel she wrote entirely alone, a somewhat incoherent work, full of contradictions and inconsistencies. She says in *Histoire de ma vie* that she composed it very quickly, 'sans projet et sans espoir, sans aucun plan' (p. 160), and in spite of being hugely popular, it was criticised by some contemporaries for its lack of unity. This, however, makes it all the more interesting for what it reveals of its complex but as yet inexperienced author, and also of the literary climate in which she lived. In many ways it is a transitional text. Although in her autobiography Sand presents it as having been written compulsively in a kind of void: 'sous l'empire d'une émotion et non d'un système' (*Vie*, p. 164) and 'ne fouillant ni dans la manière des autres ni dans ma propre individualité pour le sujet et les types' (*Vie*, p. 160), traces are evident in it of her own experiences and of the many different fictional traditions which she had inherited. It is also one of the first novels to be praised for its realism, thus foreshadowing the literary movement which was to dominate the fiction of the rest of the nineteenth century; indeed, it stands on the brink of an extraordinary flowering of the novel form in the 1830s, which established fiction as the main literary genre of the period.

This flowering had begun in the eighteenth century with the immense popularity of the *roman de mœurs* and its depiction of the decadent, aristocratic society of the ancien régime, apparently largely preoccupied with intrigue and seduction. Written by both men and women, such stories tended to follow a similar pattern of choice, pursuit and seduction, followed by marriage and abandonment, though writers like Madame Riccoboni and Madame de Charrière gave a different slant to the same plot, stressing feeling rather than calculation and sensation, and indirectly questioning the conventional narratives of male power and female submission. The depiction in *Indiana* of the frivolity of Parisian high society in the late years of the Restoration has much in common with such representations, and the character of Raymon, in his serial pursuit of Noun, Indiana herself and Laure de Nangy, is strongly reminiscent of the heroes of Laclos and Crébillon *fils*. Early in the work he is explicitly compared to Lovelace from Samuel Richardson's *Clarissa*, a seminal text for the eighteenth-century *roman de mœurs* (79).

Already within the period, however, we see signs of a reaction to these cynical, worldly narratives in such idealist writers as Jean-Jacques Rousseau and Bernardin de Saint-Pierre. Béatrice Didier sees something of Rousseau's Saint-Preux and Milord Édouard from *La Nouvelle Héloïse* in Sand's Ralph (368), but by far the most obvious influence on *Indiana* is that of Bernardin's *Paul et Virginie* (see 77). The île Bourbon in the Indian Ocean (now called La Réunion) provides the idyllic setting in both works for the natural paradise far from the corruption of the world where a boy and girl can grow up together in solitude and innocence and where sex is seen as a desecration. Indiana's bedroom after her marriage is nostalgically decorated with prints from *Paul et Virginie* and dominated by a portrait of Ralph, her childhood companion on the island. However, Sand's Bourbon is already to some extent contaminated by colonialism and patriarchy and Ralph's and Indiana's final retreat high up in the remote valley of Bernica is explicitly compared in the book's final words to a 'chaumière indienne' (344), the title of another, more exotic work by Bernardin which describes the secluded dwelling of an Indian pariah living totally alone in harmony with nature. So these two opposing fictional traditions from the eighteenth century reappear some sixty years later in the contrasting figures of Raymon and Ralph, and in the opposing spaces of Paris and Bernica, the worldly and the natural, the real and the ideal.

A more recent influence on Sand were the personal novels of the early part of the nineteenth century, works such as Chateaubriand's *René* (1802) and Senancour's *Oberman* (1804); she compares herself with the protagonist of the former in her

autobiography. These texts gave expression to the so-called
'mal du siècle', that state of melancholy and alienation induced
in young men by the political turmoils of the previous years,
which had brutally destroyed the eighteenth-century world in
which they had had their place and their role. Isabelle Hoog
Naginski points out the similarities between the opening scene
of *Indiana*, the three main characters brooding silently by the
fireside in a provincial *château* on a sombre, autumn evening,
and certain passages of Chateaubriand's *Mémoires d'outre-
tombe*, although Sand could not have read these at the time. An
important development, however, as Naginski goes on to
indicate (p. 58), is that the central character whose malaise is to
be investigated is now a woman rather than a man; until then,
so abstract and elevated a state of mind had been generally
associated with the male sex, which alone was thought capable
of such intense self-contemplation. The few women writers
within the genre had also adopted the male perspective, and it
is the hero's voice that we hear, the woman still only being
allowed the role of ideal mistress and mysterious muse whose
story we can only guess at; we find traces of this tradition in
Sand's *Mauprat*, written a generation later. Even the
celebrated Madame de Staël held back from making her
exceptional heroine Corinne the main voice of the text of that
name; the action is largely seen through Lord Nelvil, the
melancholy Englishman (not unlike Sand's Ralph) who falls in
love with her and whose angst permeates the work. Only in
Madame de Duras's little-known novel *Ourika* (1821) is a
woman's alienated consciousness the focus of the narrative,
but her alienation is social not metaphysical, since unlike
Indiana she is black and therefore excluded from the
conventional woman's position for which, again unlike
Indiana, she yearns. Her story is also framed, narrated for her
by a male doctor.

By the early 1830s such intensely personal narratives were
being replaced by panoramic visions of a 'real' society within
which an individual's experience was set, as for example in
Stendhal's *Le Rouge et le Noir* (1831). The historical novels of
Walter Scott were undoubtedly an important influence here,
but even more crucial was the rapidly changing world of the
1830s, which saw the growth of capitalism, expanding
urbanisation and the rise of the bourgeoisie. The realist project
is a response to this new world and an attempt to come to grips

with it; it is also a reaction against the earlier, melodramatic and populist *roman noir*, with its love of the macabre and fantastic, its Gothic imagery of ruined castles, graveyards and wild landscapes. The emphasis shifted from the sentimental or supernatural to the worldly and material: plots came down to earth, characters were more active and engaged, and descriptions of settings increasingly filled out with realistic detail. Adultery joined courtship and seduction as a favourite theme, since its implications and consequences were inevitably social as well as sentimental, and the adulterous woman (it mattered much less if it was a man) was largely seen, by Balzac for example, as a destructive and either tragic or sinister figure, transgressive of the rules of patriarchy. The objective, omniscient narrator of such rich and diverse worlds, brimful of moral significance, was necessarily male since it required the knowledge and authority associated with a man to persuade the reader of their truth. This explains the choice of a male narrator by George Sand (or Aurore Dudevant, as she was then) when she told the story of the unhappy Indiana against the background of the years 1827-1832.

Such, then, is the literary context in which *Indiana* was conceived and written, and it is the new realism of the novel which was most appreciated by its readers: 'C'est bien la vie, la société comme nous les connaissons,' comments an anonymous reviewer (*La Quotidienne*, 26 September 1832). Sainte-Beuve, in a review article on *Indiana* and *Valentine*, agrees:

> ... un monde vrai, vivant, nôtre, à cent lieues des scènes historiques et des lambeaux de Moyen Âge [...,] des mœurs, des personnages comme il en existe autour de nous, un langage naturel, des scènes d'un encadrement familier, des passions violentes, non communes, mais sincèrement éprouvées ou observées [...]. (360-1)

He does have his reservations, however, and goes on to point out and condemn the unconvincing idealism of the end, 'le reste qui semble d'invention presque pure'. He particularly praises the realistic portrayal of Raymon, as opposed to Ralph whom he sees as a caricature at the beginning and a total fabrication by the end. He approves of the characterization of Indiana in spite of her unworldliness (again until the end), while drawing attention to the difference between her romantic idealism and the corruption of the rest of society.

This of course is the main twist that Sand gives to the adultery plots of her realist contemporaries. Her adulterous wife is neither voluptuous nor depraved; indeed, since she appears almost frigid, and no adulterous act is actually committed, she could hardly be seen as a social danger. She has much more in common with the idealistic, Romantic hero of the earlier *romans personnels* than with Balzac's Madame de Restaud, for example, for her view of love is unbelievably ethereal. It seems that here Sand is deliberately going against realist, 'masculine' convention, agreeing with her heroine in defending the feminine idealism of what Raymon dismisses as 'romans à l'usage des femmes de chambre' (**217**) with their naïvely sentimental characters, romantic plots and happy endings. In this way the novel brings together two opposing modes, realism and idealism, the social and the personal, objective and subjective, oppositions which, as we have seen, have their origin both in the different literary traditions that Sand inherited and also in her own confused experiences and androgynous personality. As reviewer Jacques Lerond put it in the *Chronique de la Quinzaine* of 31 May 1832, hinting at a collaboration with Jules Sandeau by now no longer practised:

> On dirait que cette étoffe brillante mais sans harmonie, est l'œuvre de deux ouvriers bien distincts [...], qu'une main de jeune homme en a serré le tissu fort et grossier, qu'une main de femme y a brodé des fleurs de soie et d'or.

(ii) Narrative Voice

As well as being perplexed by the incompatibility of modes in *Indiana*, critics have also pointed out the contradictory nature of the narrative voice. This is a particularly crucial issue, since the narrator dominates the text; the story is mediated entirely through him, and his opinions constantly colour our view of the characters and their behaviour. He takes great pains to authenticate his narrative. We are all part of the same world, narrator, reader and characters: Raymon has written political pamphlets which we may have read; we have at least all known young men like him. We have wondered about Noun's death and concluded like the narrator that it was suicide: 'Il est à peu près prouvé pour le lecteur et pour moi que cette infortunée s'est jetée dans la rivière par désespoir' **(124)** We are constantly addressed directly—'Que voulez-vous!'; 'Vous savez que...'; 'Permettez-moi de..'; 'Vous verrez pour combien de temps'—as the narrator sets up a complicity with us which encourages us to suspend our disbelief, enter with him into the world of the novel and accept it as fact not fiction. Indeed, the first version of *Indiana* was peppered with such immediate appeals, which commented not only on the events of the plot but also on the narrator's storytelling itself, on how certain scenes should be described (discreetly rather than flamboyantly), what must be included and what left to the reader's imagination. For the second edition, Sand clearly felt these were too intrusive and cut most of them out.

So the narrator presents himself as a character in his own right, on the same level as Ralph or Raymon and with a personality and opinions like theirs. The difficulty however is to build up a consistent and convincing picture of this extra persona. There is no doubt that he is not the author, although it is also his voice that speaks in the 1832 preface as Sand's impersonation extends beyond the text itself. He is clearly male, and may speak directly on behalf of the male sex: 'C'est la violence de nos désirs, la précipitation de notre amour qui nous rend stupides auprès des femmes' **(83)**. He is patronising to women, making generalisations about their weakness, foolishness and sentimentality: 'La femme est imbécile par nature' **(251)**; 'l'amour, c'est la vertu de la femme' **(279)**; 'la femme est faite ainsi' **(274)**. For most of the time he is cynical and worldly-wise, mystified by the impassive Ralph and partly defending Raymon's callous treatment of poor, illiterate Noun, excusing his pragmatism and cowardice, and sympathising with his love for Indiana. Raymon is portrayed as 'un homme supérieur dans la société' **(128)**, indeed a prize specimen: 'un homme capable de folie en amour est un prodige assez rare, et que les femmes ne dédaignent pas' **(84)**. Yet there is something double-edged about these compliments, and the narrator also goes out of his way to be fair to the tyrannical and insensitive Delmare, who is not 'un méchant homme' **(271)**. The rough soldier has been brutalised by camp life but could have been changed and softened by a more understanding wife. He truly loves Indiana and is reduced to tears by his own violent treatment of her. There is much sympathy of course for Indiana too, for her loneliness and need for love, but there is also a

recognition that she is impulsive and deluded. The tone is one
of urbane tolerance which judges nobody too harshly, where
everybody has their qualities and their faults; 'elle avait les
defauts de ses qualités, et lui les qualités de ses défauts' (210)
On occasion, however, the mask, if it is a mask, drops; the
language becomes suddenly direct and impassioned as the
narrative voice turns against that society of which, like
Raymon, it seemed a part. The reader is required to reject its
cynicism and worldliness and to flee into the country, seeking
out the alternative values of rural peace and domesticity:
'Prenez vos pénates et transportez-les au fond des bois, au sein
des landes désertes. Là seulement, et tout au plus, l'homme des
petites villes vous laissera en repos' (211); and again: 'Heureux
habitants des campagnes, s'il est encore des campagnes en
France, fuyez, fuyez la politique, et lisez *Peau d'âne* en famille'
(171) Nursery tales are preferable to such sophisticated
narratives as we are reading now, paradoxically seen here as
dangerous and corrupting. At this point, the narrator seems
much closer to Sand herself: he is on the side of the victimised
and oppressed, of Noun and her mistress, who have little
command of language and cannot play the social game. He
criticises Raymon's eloquence, a 'reine prostituée' (130) that is
the object of idolatry rather than of love, and indeed is scathing
about a whole society which trusts to words rather than deeds:
'Le plus honnête des hommes est celui qui pense et qui agit le
mieux, mais le plus puissant est celui qui sait le mieux écrire et
parler' (130) He praises the dignity of silence. In her quiet
resistance to her husband, Indiana is no longer a weak and
foolish woman but has 'la dignité d'un roi' (208), and the
narrator is entirely in sympathy with her desire for freedom.
This leaves the reader somewhat perplexed, wondering if this
is the same person who elsewhere seemed to understand and
accept the rules of society. There is no suggestion that it is not,
but Sand makes little attempt to explain or resolve the
discrepancy between the two incompatible sets of values.

The contradiction in narrative voice is even more glaring at
the end of the novel when the narrating *je* suddenly appears in
person at the île Bourbon, makes the acquaintance of Ralph
and Indiana, now settled in the valley of Bernica, and hears
from Ralph the story of their lives as we have just been reading
it: 'sir Ralph, me faisant asseoir à côté de lui sur un banc dans le
jardin, me raconta son histoire jusqu'à l'endroit où nous

l'avons laissée dans le précédent chapitre' (339). The assumption is that the narrator then wrote it down for the benefit of the rest of society. This epilogue motivates the text, describing its origin as well as recounting its conclusion. It is similar to the prologue in Benjamin Constant's *Adolphe*, for example, whose function is to arouse the reader's curiosity and prepare him for the kind of text he is about to read. Placed at the end, it appears more like an afterthought, particularly as it reverses the conclusion which we have just read; we find that Ralph and Indiana have not killed themselves, as we had been led to expect, but are living happily in social isolation in the very valley into which they had apparently plunged to their death. Sand dedicates this conclusion to her friend, Jules Néraud, who lived near her in the Berry, in order to thank him for the help his intimate knowledge of the île Bourbon had given her, and this is even more confusing since the dedication 'À J. Néraud' is clearly in Sand's own voice and not in that of any fictional narrator. What is most confusing of all, though, is the discrepancy between the first-person narrator of the conclusion and the apparently omniscient narrator of the rest of the novel. The later one is young and naïve, modest and easily impressed, eager to learn from others; he has few social skills, is quick to doubt himself and bursts into tears when he has to leave Ralph's and Indiana's retreat. He appears so different from the confident, all-knowing narrative voice to which we have become accustomed that, for Robert Godwin-Jones (p. 303, n. 15), they are not the same person. This, though, would leave the conclusion even more disconnected from the main part of the book, and would simply replace one problem with another: what, then, is he doing in the story at all?

Critics have suggested various hypotheses in order to make sense of this contradictory, inconsistent narrating figure. The most common of these, advanced by Godwin-Jones (pp. 15-16), Kathryn Crecelius and Sandy Petrey is that Sand intended the male voice of the narrator to be read ironically; his misogyny is so extreme, argues Petrey, as to be a kind of parody of a male view which it is inconceivable we should take seriously (pp. 136; 144). Thus, rather than impersonating a male narrator, Sand is implicitly questioning his reliability: the reader may be persuaded that the opposite of what he says is the truth. For Crecelius (pp. 59; 63), she is using a 'male voice but with a female perspective'; 'the female voice has gone underground', and we are convinced of its rightness almost without realizing it, a much more effective way of encouraging a male readership towards a feminist point of view than if it were stated directly. Indeed Peter Dayan sees a similar tension within many of Sand's novels, between the male narrator who writes from within the establishment in terms of its power structures, and the implicit message that emerges from the characters and events themselves and that often coincides with a 'feminine' view: 'J'irai jusqu'à dire que la cohérence romanesque, chez Sand, est le produit du regard masculin; mais l'intérêt du roman tient à un certain alliage de réel, de liberté, d'imprévu qui mine cette cohérence et ce regard' (1, p. 43). These theories are very compelling: it does indeed seem that the only way we can satisfactorily read such statements from the novel as 'la femme est imbécile par nature' is ironically, and the irony certainly adds interest to the person of the narrator himself. It does not account, however, for the inconsistencies within the narrative voice, the discrepancy between such sexism and his fair-mindedness elsewhere, and particularly his occasional passionate defence of the weak; nor does it solve the problem of the two different narrators. Moreover, it is impossible to know for certain when to read the narrator ironically and when not. When the irony is palpable, is it intentional (on his part) or unconscious? This theory effectively exonerates Sand from any male chauvinism but does nothing to make the text more coherent.

Dayan has put forward a rather different hypothesis, which accounts for the inconsistencies of the narrative voice but which some readers may find somewhat far-fetched. His suggestion is that the narrator of all the main part of the text is Ralph himself, who, in a kind of male exchange which excludes the woman, Indiana, tells their story directly to the young, first-person narrator of the conclusion, who then writes it down as it has been recounted to him. Thus 'in the first four parts, the narrator is giving us Ralph's version and interpretation of events, from Ralph's point of view, though in the third person; whereas in the conclusion, he is speaking in his own voice' (2, p. 155). This successfully deals with the problem of the two narrators, and is convincing in that the contradiction between the primary one's patronizing view of women and his sympathy with the disadvantaged would be resolved. These two attitudes do coexist within Ralph's 'masculine idealism'. It is true too that Ralph's strong sense of justice could well lead him to give the balanced, fair-minded view of both Delmare and Raymon which we have already noticed. It is more difficult to explain away the unsympathetic picture he gives of himself at the beginning and the emphasis on his inscrutability, although Dayan suggests that this is a way of building up suspense which makes the final revelation, when he is allowed to speak for himself (within the text rather than as narrator), all the more dramatic. The novel, then, would trace 'his acquisition of a voice' (2, p. 160). A reader may still not find it easy to reconcile the alienated, tormented figure of Ralph, as we know him by the end, with the cynical worldly wisdom of some of the narrator's earlier statements, nor with his self-conscious attitude to his own narration—although the theory certainly accounts for the very direct, conversational tone. We may also wonder why, if this was her intention, Sand did not make it clear to us since her narrative would undoubtedly have gained in coherence if she had.

Perhaps some of these explanations are too ingenious; they ascribe to Sand a narrative and linguistic sophistication which it is unlikely she possessed at this early stage in her writing career. She is still feeling her way, unable yet to accommodate satisfactorily her personal convictions within the realist mode which was the popular literary style of the time and which she therefore adopted as her own. She certainly takes on some of the mannerisms of Balzac, for example his intrusive narrative voice, with its many generalisations on social and human types and its moralising tone. Indeed when her friend Delatouche read the first part of *Indiana*, he described it as pure Balzac; 'Allons! c'est un pastiche; école de Balzac!', although he changed his mind after reading the whole novel (358). Balzac was Sand's close friend, she admired his books and they had many literary discussions together; he even portrayed her sympathetically as the novelist Camille Maupin in *Béatrix*. It is natural that she should have imitated him, but less obvious that she should have done so with any ironic intention. Is she not simply adopting the voice of patriarchy, of realist narrative fiction as it was at the time, even though it sits oddly with her feminine idealism, her instinctive sympathy with oppressed women (particularly in marriage), which are also at the root of the novel? In *Indiana* the incompatibility remains; five years later, in *Mauprat*, Sand has abandoned the realist mode and the narrator is clearly part of the fiction, so that we know from the beginning that we cannot trust him implicitly. Sand's difficulty in handling the narrator in *Indiana* perhaps betrays her ambiguous position in the literary establishment of the time: the professional writer needed to be within it, but the woman with a woman's sympathies was necessarily outside it.

Characterisation

In her discussion of the composition of *Indiana* in her autobiography, Sand makes a clear distinction between characters as they exist in real life (herself, for example) and the characters of a novel. The former may be as inconsistent and inconsequential as they like; the latter must follow a certain logic, represent particular principles and, most importantly, submit to some degree of idealisation: 'Je suis trop romanesque pour avoir vu une héroïne de roman dans mon miroir. Je ne me suis jamais trouvée ni assez belle, ni assez aimable, ni assez logique dans l'ensemble de mon caractère et de mes actions pour prêter à la poésie ou à l'intérêt' (*Vie*, p. 160). This was her response to those of her contemporaries who insisted on seeing in *Indiana* the story of her own experiences, and indeed we may well agree that this narrative of a young woman unhappily married to an insensitive, tyrannical former soldier who is older than her does seem drawn in part from Aurore Dupin's own marriage to Casimir Dudevant. Yet, as we saw above (in 'Context'), the characters of her novel also owe much to previous literary figures: Valmont, Paul and Virginie, or René. As Sand says, they are to some extent types rather than real people as a result. Perhaps it was not so much her own self and the actual persons of her husband and lovers that Sand used as material for her fiction, but rather the intimate convictions that her experiences had bred in her, her hatred of oppression, her belief in justice and equality, and her idealised vision of the perfect partnership. It is these which are responsible for the transformations she effects in the literary influences of her time. Sometimes, as we shall see, the inherited type and the personal ideal are not easy to reconcile; they may sit oddly together, particularly in the characters of Indiana and Ralph, her most original creations.

Both of these possess opposing and apparently contradictory features, as Sand tried to adapt the models she felt she still needed to make them express her personal vision.

Her characters arrange themselves very neatly into a series of pairs and triangles so that, as in Laclos's *Les Liaisons dangereuses* or in a Marivaux play, we see the original couples evolving through various triangular relationships (and the death of two of the partners) into a set of different couples. Indiana moves from Delmare to Ralph by way of Raymon; Ralph begins as the third person in a domestic triangle, then becomes the central figure in the final pairing with Indiana; Raymon proceeds from Noun to Indiana and then to Laure de Nangy. One is reminded of the ordered movements of figures in a ballet as characters change places in sequence. Of course such changes of disposition happen frequently in real life, but here they all occur within the closed circle of a very small group of people, as in the cast of a classical tragedy, rather than with the randomness of the everyday. Moreover, the group itself is almost entirely organised in terms of parallels and opposites. Ralph and Raymon fight over Indiana like antithetical figures of good and evil, the guardian angel and the seductive demon. Indiana and Noun are clearly both opposites and interchangeable. The three men represent the three contrasting political stances of the time; even the minor figure of Laure de Nangy is in every way the reverse of Indiana. In the opening descriptions of the novel, figures are explicitly set against each other as opposing physical and mental types: Ralph's robust, youthful features 'juraient avec les cheveux grisonnants, le teint flétri et la rude physionomie du patron [Delmare]' (**51**), and their two faces as they bend over the fainting Raymon are 'si différentes [...,] l'une pâle et contractée par le dépit, l'autre calme et insignifiante comme à l'ordinaire' (**69**). Noun's physical vigour and healthy good looks 'effaçai[en]t de beaucoup, par sa beauté resplendissante, la beauté pâle et frêle de Madame Delmare' (**60**). Again the symmetries are rather those of art than life.

Naginski demonstrates convincingly how each character is defined by a certain kind of language, thus conforming to a particular linguistic as well as physical and mental type: 'Each of the principal characters speaks a language that embodies the role he or she plays' (p. 63) The comparison with the theatre here emphasises again the studied literariness of the

representations. The different political stances of the three men
are revealed through different modes of speech: Raymon, the
aristocratic royalist, is fluent and persuasive, Delmare is
bogged down in the over-simple clichés of Napoleonic
militarism, and Ralph's rough candour bears witness to his
deeply-felt liberal idealism. Raymon is the most eloquent; he is
not only a practised politician but also a skilled seducer who
manipulates the vocabulary and rhetoric of Romanticism with
quite as much effectiveness—to the extent that he even
deceives himself. It is his eloquence that produces his passion
rather than his passion that makes him eloquent, says the
narrator, in an open condemnation of the man of the world.
Naginski (like Dayan) sees Ralph's transformation in the
course of the novel as largely linguistic; he develops from the
clumsy, inarticulate outsider of the early part of the text, whom
we cannnot fathom because he cannot speak for himself, to the
fluent Messiah of the end who recounts his inner life to Indiana
in the most poetic and dramatic of styles. Thus the novel truly
presents Ralph's development as his 'acquisition of a voice'; he
undergoes no fundamental change of character in the novel,
but since it is largely through their speech that these characters
define themselves, it is only by the end that we have any real
sense of who Ralph is. It seems, too, that in him the gift of
speech is not a corruption of authenticity, as it is in Raymon but
an expression of the true self, although the reader clearly
recognises in Ralph's confession just as much of a borrowed
literary style, full of reminiscences from the Bible, as in
Raymon's language of seduction. Noun's innocence, on the
other hand, is guaranteed by her lack of a voice; her letter to
Raymon is movingly sincere precisely because she is illiterate.
Indiana too is characterised by her mutism in society although,
unlike Noun, she can write, and in her long letter to Raymon
and in her diary, both written in the privacy of her room on the
île Bourbon, she effectively gives voice to all her most deeply
held desires and convictions.

Of course, the characters of *Indiana* are social, as well as
physical, mental and linguistic types. Sand follows Balzac in
embedding them in their period, explaining their dispositions
by the effect that history has had on them. This is perhaps most
obvious in the peripheral figures of the two old ladies,
Madame de Carvajal (Indiana's aunt) and Madame de
Ramière (Raymon's mother). Because of their minor role in the

action, they are relatively simplified and are important largely through their effect on the two main characters. Again, they appear clearly as opposites, the good and the bad. Madame de Ramière 'était une de ces femmes qui ont traversé des époques si différentes, que leur esprit a pris toute la souplesse de leur destinée, qui se sont enrichies de l'expérience du malheur' (78); the turbulence of her life has made her tolerant and compassionate to others, even to her selfish and wayward son. In a small personal touch, Sand attributes to her the last words that her own grandmother had spoken to her on her deathbed: 'Vous perdez votre meilleure amie' (265), a sure mark of her sympathy. Madame de Carvajal, on the contrary, thinks only of her own survival and 'achalandage pour sa société' (214); ambitious and scheming, she adapts to each new, passing regime, and protects Indiana only in so far as she can benefit from the relationship. When Indiana breaks the rules of society by leaving her husband to go to her lover, she casts her off without a second thought. Thus, the political instability of the forty years before 1830 produced two antithetical types: the one thinking only of others, the other only of herself.

Raymon is the character who is most closely and explicitly linked to his time. He is entirely a product of his society; he has taken on its ways of thinking and cannot live long far from the public eye. He skilfully adapts his political views, hedging his bets in order to ensure his position. 'Il avait fait de la politique l'âme de toutes ses pensées' (260). He understands the cynicism of all around him and makes use of it when he can; he retrieves his position after 1830 by marrying Laure de Nangy, a wealthy heiress, whose money comes from the new industrialism of the early nineteenth century. Indeed, Petrey sees not only his politics but his very masculinity as socially constructed; romance is inextricably involved with class and social position: 'When men and women come together in Indiana, the sparks still fly. The novel's specificity is ascribing the heat to ideology rather than physiology' (p. 138). Raymon loves in Indiana not so much the real woman as her aristocratic manners and the feminine luxury of her room, and instinctively turns away from Noun when he sees her in her maid's dress. 'What [gendered features] are comes not from anatomical attributes but from received ideas' (p. 145). The power structures of society are carried over into love relationships and marriage; one person must be in control and the other (usually, but not always, the

woman) must submit. Raymon clearly thinks in these terms of
Indiana; he wants her as a slave to feed his pride. His aim is to
possess her and if he cannot possess her directly, he will at least
penetrate her bedroom, look into all her secrets: 'il ouvrit ses
livres, feuilleta ses albums' (107). His love for her is fed by his
narcissism and largely controlled by his reason; he calculates
the different stages of her seduction very much as Valmont
plots the fall of Madame de Tourvel in *Les Liaisons
dangereuses*, although Indiana, as we shall see, several times
refuses the role allotted her, and Raymon's plans do not
succeed. In his vanity, he cannot bear to be made a fool of, and
it is the macabre trick which Indiana plays on him when she
pretends the dead Noun's hair is her own (192) that finally kills
his love for her. In the end, his need for public status becomes
stronger even than his private self-respect, and in his marriage
to Laure de Nangy it is she who is in control, since she has the
money that guarantees social position in the world after 1830.

It is Raymon who benefits most from the narrator's attempt
at a balanced, worldly view since he incarnates that male
world of which the narrator needs to be part if he is to be taken
seriously. The result is that he is portrayed with a detail which
brings him vividly to life: he is a type (the type of the man of the
world), but Sand develops fully the complexities and
contradictions of such a type, whose faults are most often the
result of that very worldliness to which he also owes his
intelligence and charm. Sainte-Beuve felt that he was the most
effective of Sand's creations because he was the most lifelike
and the most interesting. This appears paradoxical since it is
likely that Sand put the least of her self and her experiences
into the character of Raymon; he owes his vitality less to real
life than to the number and power of his models, to the great
novels of seduction of the eighteenth century, (going back even
earlier to the duc de Nemours in *La Princesse de Clèves*) which
explored such a type with unsurpassed subtlety and
penetration. Sand was following in a long tradition which she
wished not to question or subvert but to recreate, as part of her
depiction of a society against which her more original figures
might stand. So we find in Raymon none of the odd
inconsistencies of Indiana and Ralph. He is at the same time
the most convincing of all the characters and the most
stereotyped.

Laure de Nangy, as Raymon's female counterpart, is a more original creation, although she may owe something to Laclos's Madame de Merteuil. She is the product, as Petrey points out (pp. 140-1), of a world that has moved on, that same world which rejected the old royalism and exploded into the July Revolution. A daughter of the now impoverished aristocracy, she has been adopted by a rich industrialist whose new money she inherits. She combines the beauty and polish of the old regime with the power of the new: 'une femme de son [Raymon's] rang à la tête d'une belle fortune plébéienne' (288). She is also a woman of her time through her pragmatism and materialism; she will do whatever she needs in order to succeed. She believes in nothing: in her drawings she parodies the artificial preciosity of the old world, but she also mocks the Romantic melodrama of Indiana's gesture as she falls at Raymon's feet at their final meeting. The roles are now reversed; the man is dominated by the woman, wealth creates power. The future belongs to her, which of course is why Raymon marries her. Yet we sense that this is not Sand's ideal of the new woman. Laure has a cool head but no heart, and Sand's feminism depends on the heart, on the importance of love, not on female control for its own sake. Laure is an interesting experiment but Sand's later great female figures— Edmée, Jeanne, Consuelo, Fadette—take a quite different path.

Some third of the way through the novel, Sand interrupts her narrative (as Balzac so often does) in order to give a portrait of Raymon, followed immediately by one of Delmare. They come near the beginning of Part Two, after the death of Noun, when the action enters a second phase. Whereas Raymon appears as a consistent and credible character, the picture of Delmare which emerges is more confused: the passage begins with an ironic denunciation of society's tolerance of male tyranny within the family: 'Pourvu qu'il respecte religieusement la vie et la bourse de ses concitoyens, on ne lui demande pas compte d'autre chose. Il peut battre sa femme, maltraiter ses gens, ruiner ses enfants, cela ne regarde personne' (132). We find exactly the same condemnation of the laws of marriage, expressed in similarly striking language, in Sand's autobiography, which suggests strongly that the figure of Delmare owes much to her own husband. All her accumulated bitterness surfaces here, and is made even clearer

in the highly individualised description of Delmare which
follows, and which we sense is fuelled by her own memories of
Casimir—his contempt for feminine delicacy that he does not
understand, his physical strength and stupidity, combined with
'une susceptibilité ombrageuse' (133), which make of him the
worst kind of tyrant since his only way of imposing himself is
through fear. Then, as though she realises that the tone has
become too subjective, too emotional, Sand reverts in the next
paragraph to the style of the objective narrator and shifts the
blame for Delmare's brutality away from his person and on to
his training and experiences as a soldier in Napoleon's army;
'Ce fut la faute du siècle plutôt que la leur' (133). This leads on
to a veiled attack on Napoleon's militarism, which Sand
abandons suddenly at the end of the paragraph as the address
becomes too personal again: 'mais je sais qu'il est défendu de
parler impartialement de ces choses; je me tais, la postérité les
jugera' (134). She then moves into a more balanced description
of Delmare's character, 'confiant comme un enfant,
soupçonneux comme un despote' (134), which lays the blame
for the Delmares' unhappy marriage equally on the shoulders
of husband and wife: 'Madame Delmare doutait trop du cœur
de son mari; il n'était que dur, et elle le jugea cruel' (135).

In other parts of the book, when Delmare speaks and acts
for himself, it is the real man, Casimir Dudevant, that we see
again, the man whose presence the author had felt as a block to
her freedom and who once threatened her with a gun. In the
novel, he takes every opportunity to exercise his power, on his
wife's dog if not on her, eventually stamping on her face with
his boot on discovering her private diary (269). Thus there is a
clear tension in the text between the realist narrator's search
for an objective style which would set Delmare up as a certain
social type for our information and understanding, and the real
woman's passionate and partial anger against the husband she
felt had treated her unfairly. Indeed, it is into this
representation of a man's relationship with his wife, however
caricatured, that Sand appears to have put most of her own
experience, while at the same time trying to conform to the
realist conventions within which she was working.

Noun is the least individualised and fleshed out of all the
characters; she is a type and a symbol rather than a reality. She
is four times a victim: as woman, creole, maid, and finally as
seduced and pregnant mistress. She is totally dependent on

others, on her mistress and her lover, and when they both fail
her there is nothing left for her to do but to disappear; even her
death is passive rather than active as she allows herself to be
carried away by the river and drowns. Her suicide is not
described directly, the fact is simply assumed, and two months
later, it is as though she had never existed: 'Deux mois se sont
écoulés. Il n'y a rien de changé au Lagny' **(120)**. She drowns a
third of the way through the text, and yet she cannot be
forgotten; her ghost remains to haunt the rest of the book as a
reminder to the other characters of man's (and woman's)
injustice to woman. The reasonable and practical Raymon goes
into a cold sweat whenever her name is mentioned, and
Indiana is several times tempted to imitate her fate.

For Noun is also a counterpart to Indiana. She is physically
her opposite, 'grande, forte, brillante de santé, vive, alerte, et
pleine de sang créole ardent et passionné' **(60)**, and in Marilyn
Yalom's opinion is an expression of Sand's 'repressed Self',
which 'in literature [...] is allowed to have its day' (p. 24). Doris
Kadish (p. 28) compares her to Rochester's insane wife Bertha
in *Jane Eyre* (said by her husband to be descended from a mad
and alcoholic female, 'the Creole' [Chapter 26]), but without
her animal violence; Patricia Thomson too (p. 74) notes these
parallels. Noun represents female sexuality and, with all her
natural innocence, is potentially a threat to society's peace of
mind and must be eliminated as soon as she starts to assert her
rights. She represents that side of Indiana, the sexual side,
which her mistress cannot acknowledge and which she seems
completely to ignore. Noun is her *alter ego*, her 'sœur de lait'
(60) with whom she shared the wet-nurse's breast on the île
Bourbon **(157)** and whom she brought back with her to France.
They are courted by the same man in the same bedroom; they
have the same head of luxuriant black hair which symbolises
their femininity, hair explicitly presented as interchangeable
when Indiana offers Noun's hair to Raymon as her own. But
Noun's hair is dead, while Indiana is alive, and Noun's death is
a constant example to Indiana of what might happen to her.
Noun's reality is largely literary; she only exists as the
archetypal victim of society, and as the tragic face of Indiana.

Since Indiana's name (significantly, only her Christian
name) is the title of the book, we assume that it is her story we
are to hear. The novel appears as a *roman personnel* like *René*,
Adolphe, and *Corinne* rather than the more socially oriented

Le Rouge et le Noir, Eugénie Grandet or *Madame Bovary*.
Indiana suffers from the typical Romantic malady: 'Aussi elle se
mourait. Un mal inconnu dévorait sa jeunesse. Elle était sans
force et sans sommeil. Les médecins lui cherchaient en vain une
désorganisation apparente, il n'en existait pas' (89). Typically
she sits brooding beside the fire, gazing into the dying embers,
like Chateaubriand's René on the edge of the volcano. Yet
Indiana's melancholy is not purely metaphysical, as is that of
her male counterparts; it stems at least partly from her position
in society, from the fact that she is a woman, powerless and
trapped, so the novel must have a social dimension in order for
her state of mind to be fully understood. Her condition might be
cured if society were to change, hence the happy ending when
Ralph and she together succeed in creating a new partnership
in their own image. René's story could never have a happy
ending since his angst has no earthly remedy. This is the first
difference between Indiana and at least one of her models. By
setting her depiction of (female) 'mal du siècle' against a
precise social background and so giving it a possible reason and
perhaps a cure, Sand has moved the personal novel on a stage
and satisfied several different kinds of reader, the worldly and
the sentimental, the male as well as the female.

It is perhaps the contradictions of Indiana's character which
fascinate us most. In many ways, she is a typical Romantic
heroine. Pale, since she is a Caucasian, and beautiful,
apparently submissive and dependent, she lives for love and at
times takes pleasure in abasing herself before her lover. She is
easily taken in, sees life as a novel and needs a protector in
order to survive. Because of her creole nurturing by absorption
of indigenous milk (157) and local customs, she has also the
attraction of the exotic (as revealed by her name, which
reminds us of the faraway Indian Ocean from where 'la belle
Indienne' [81] has come), although in other ways her alien
background simply reinforces her feminine inferiority. She is
barely educated, having spent her lonely childhood running
wild on the beaches and in the mountains of her native island
with only Ralph as her teacher. She has animistic as well as
Christian beliefs 'Madame Delmare avait toutes les
superstitions d'une créole, nerveuse et maladive' (59). She lacks
social skills: 'Une Française, une personne du monde, n'eût pas
perdu la tête dans une situation si délicate; mais Indiana
n'avait pas d'*usage*' (144).

But on the other hand, she is strong and courageous when defying her tyrannical husband, often by a dignified silence. She has 'une volonté de fer, une force de résistance incalculable contre tout ce qui tendait à l'opprimer' (88) A crisis brings out the best in her; she can act decisively and with a moral courage which at one point the narrator says is characteristic of women rather than men. She is clever enough to present her flight to Raymon's room as a deliberate bid for freedom rather than an attempt to join her lover (as it really was). She can be so lucid and articulate in her defiance of her husband that he is left speechless: 'Je sais que je suis l'esclave et vous le seigneur. La loi de ce pays vous a fait mon maître. [...] Vous avez le droit du plus fort, et la société vous le confirme; mais sur ma volonté, monsieur, vous ne pouvez rien' (232). A completely fearless huntress, she demonstrates 'un courage plus que masculin, cette sorte d'intrépidité délirante qui se manifeste parfois comme une crise nerveuse chez les êtres les plus faibles' (162).

Even more surprisingly, she appears to have worked out a system of beliefs which is religious and social as well as emotional. Her ideal of love is impossibly elevated; she demands total devotion, but without any sex. Yet her idealism is also political, and it is not clear whether she expects freedom or love from the Messiah for whom she is waiting. What is certain is that her initial motive for fleeing from the île Bourbon was a desire to love alone, away from the constraints imposed by husband and society. Only later does she think of escaping in order to join Raymon in France. It is in the letter she writes to him when she first arrives at the island that she expresses her personal creed most eloquently, opposing it to the beliefs of what she describes as a patriarchal society: 'je ne sers pas le même Dieu, mais je le sers mieux, et plus purement. Le vôtre, c'est le dieu des hommes, c'est le roi, le fondateur et l'appui de votre race; le mien, c'est le Dieu de l'univers, le créateur, le soutien et l'espoir de toutes les créatures' (248-9). She sees clearly the basic worldliness of established religion, whose function is to support the power structures of society. Her God is the God of love, the God of the poor and oppressed, the God of slaves, and of women. This is a rare moment when Indiana is allowed to articulate her personal vision, to speak for herself and probably also for her creator, and she does it with eloquence and great persuasive power, even though, as Naginski points out, her eloquence is a response to ill-treatment, defensive rather than active (p. 65). It is all the more disappointing, then, to see her retreat again into Ralph's shadow at the conclusion of the novel as he will only recount their joint story to the young narrator in her absence. She has handed over her voice to Ralph in a gesture of typical feminine submission, and she is by now so withdrawn from the public eye that for the other inhabitants of the island her very existence is 'une chose problématique' (**334**.)

So Indiana is both strong and weak, thoughtful and impulsive, articulate and silent; there is also some confusion as to how far she is typical and how far an exception. Her Romantic idealism is presented as exceptional, by herself at least: 'Savez-vous ce que c'est qu'aimer une femme comme moi?' (**147**), and the vocabulary used to describe her resistance to Raymon and Delmare—'ce sang-froid qui la rendait si remarquable dans les moments de crise' (**116**); 'une femme de l'espèce commune eût dominé cet homme d'une trempe vulgaire' (**208**)—suggests that she is not like other women, that she has a rare strength of mind and a singular sense of her own dignity. We are also encouraged to think of her honesty and simplicity as unusual and are struck by the considered idealism of her letter to Raymon (**245-51**). Yet what the narrator chooses to comment on after the quoting of this letter is not its profundity and persuasive power but the typical self-delusion of its writer, who cannot cease to believe in Raymon's love for her. Indeed, it is at this point, immediately after this example of female intelligence, that the narrator comments on the natural imbecility of all women, following this with the emphatic statement; 'Voilà ce que je vous répondrais si vous me disiez qu'Indiana est un caractère d'exception' (**251**). Sand herself plays down Indiana's difference in the preface of 1832, although here still in her male impersonation: 'Indiana, [...] c'est un type; c'est la femme, l'être faible chargé de représenter *les passions* comprimées, ou, si vous aimez mieux, supprimées par *les lois*' (**40**). The contradiction between type and exception is linked of course to all the other contradictions in the figure of Indiana, and can perhaps best be explained again by Sand's double purpose in writing the book. She needed to remain within the bounds of credibility, not depart too far from her readers' expectations of a female character in a *roman personnel* or a realist novel. Yet, as we see more clearly in *Mauprat*, she also believed in the potential power of women to change the way we think about the world, and this message already lies behind this earliest of her novels, though not yet completely disentangled from more conventional ideas of femininity. Interestingly, we find the same confusion in her autobiography with regard to her own person; she presents herself as a woman like other women, but she also stresses her difference, which she attributes to her temperament and upbringing. 'Thus Indiana's androgynous nature [...] is viewed [...] as the product of her author's "virile character", her own unstable gender identity,' as Naomi Schor says (2, p. x). In *Indiana*, Sand is trying to have it both ways: reflect the present but also prepare for the future—'je cherchais encore à résoudre cet insoluble problème: *le moyen de concilier le bonheur et la dignité des individus opprimés par cette même société, sans modifier la société elle-même'* (44)—hence the over-polarised oppositions of her character, which cannot be easily resolved into a lifelike complexity.

Any difficulty we may have in making sense of the character of Indiana pales into insignificance when we look at Ralph. At least her motivations are clear, if contradictory; her emotions can be explained by her childhood and her present situation, and she fits into various recognizable categories. All this applies much less obviously to Ralph, at least until his self-revelations at the end, and even then his choice of suicide as the consummation of his relationship with Indiana remains surprising. Indeed, readers have been very divided in their assessment of his role in the work. As we have seen, Sainte-Beuve dismissed him as bizarre and unrealistic, whereas Naginski and Dayan see him as the central focus of the text. In fact, of course, these two views are not necessarily incompatible, since he is unrealistic precisely because he is the incarnation of Sand's ideal man. To begin with, he is seen from the point of view of society in the form of the worldly narrator, who cannot make any sense of him. What is he doing that first autumn evening by the fireside, sharing the domestic intimacy of husband and wife as part of what Schor calls 'a bizarre Oedipal triangle'? (2, p. xiii) He cannot be Indiana's lover (as we might at first suppose) since the scene totally lacks the tension which would normally accompany such a relationship in such a situation. The characters are all bored and depressed. His face is insipid and expressionless; he speaks 'd'un ton monotone et lourd comme ses pensées' (**58**) Later he is characterised as the type of the phlegmatic, melancholy British (something like Lord Nelvil in *Corinne*) as he prepares to commit suicide on hearing the false news of Indiana's death 'avec un sang-froid vraiment britannique' (163). He is several times described as 'égoïste' (e.g. 123; 175), which could suggest self-containment, withdrawal from others as well as selfishness. He is certainly an outsider (like Indiana), having lived on the île Bourbon and in England, away from the frivolous Parisian world in which the others move. Yet he is always there, on the fringe of things, observant and impassive.

Gradually the narrator's (and our) view of him mellows. We begin to appreciate that his role is that of Indiana's protector, her guardian angel, increasingly active and necessary. We do not understand their relationship but come to expect his sudden intervention at moments of crisis when she is on the point of death. Now he is one of the 'âmes nobles' and on the boat back to the island, Indiana sees 'la paisible et bienveillante figure de Ralph qui lui souriait' (244). We realise he has a secret, 'car dans ce corps robuste, dans ce tempérament calme et réservé, fermentaient des émotions puissantes' (243), and we begin to guess what it is, although it is only much later in his final confession of the devoted love he has always felt for Indiana that it becomes clear.

On seeing Indiana's despair at the marriage of Raymon with Laure de Nangy, Ralph fully comes into his own. He develops into Sand's ideal companion, strangely sexless. He is Indiana's cousin, like a father or brother rather than lover, for we never really know whether the relationship is consummated. He has something of Corambé, the semi-divine figure imagined by Sand in her childhood to take the place of mother, father, brother, sister, and indeed (like Indiana, like Sand herself), Ralph transcends any gender categorisation. Naginski speaks of his 'androgynous' voice (p. 65), which she compares to Sand's own. He saves Indiana from despair by offering her suicide as an alternative, death rather than life, but a death which would consecrate their relationship like a spiritual marriage. In fact, of course, they do not die but live on in an ideal partnership, withdrawn from society. He is indeed the Messiah, the liberator she was expecting, although in a form for which her reading of 'romans à l'usage de femmes de chambre' (247) had not prepared her. He is Sand's most original creation, the figure into which she poured all her spiritual and emotional needs at the time. In this way, he is the focus of the entire text even though such a focus inevitably disturbs any view we may have of the novel as conventionally realistic.

(iii) Plot

In spite of the importance of Ralph as protector; mediator and finally as Messiah, when we look at the action of the novel there is no doubt that this is Indiana's story. It is her development that is central—from her melancholy longings at the beginning to her silent contentment at the end. It takes a long time for her to find herself: for much of the book, she persists in following the wrong path until she reaches a state of non-being beyond despair, from which she finally resurrects into her true identity. Since she is a woman, her search for personal fulfilment takes the form of a search for love, rather than power, wealth or fame, and the traditional structure of a quest narrative becomes also that of a romance. She cannot find happiness on her own; she needs a man to lead the way, and her conversion consists primarily in her realisation of the difference between Raymon's false charm and the genuine nobility of Ralph. Sand was not yet bold enough to invent a heroine with the strength and independence of mind to act entirely alone. But by concentrating on the development, the *Bildung,* of a woman, she does give the conventional quest narrative a new slant. She retains the idea of tests to be taken, obstacles to be surmounted but these are as much psychological as physical. For Indiana, the dragons to be slain are social opinion and her own infatuation with the wrong man. She also needs the moral strength to resist Raymon's attempts at physical seduction and Delmare's enforced imprisonment of her. Her final test is set by Ralph when he challenges her to withdraw completely from the world and agree to a joint suicide; by this time she has learned whom to trust, accepts the challenge with joy, and so earns the right to happiness at the end. As Crecelius puts it: 'She [Sand] has made the quest romance accessible to a heroine, while giving it a purely psychological and social dimension and eliminating the physical adventures' (p. 80). In fact, there are still some physical adventures, trials of Indiana's courage and determination, in particular an ordeal by water, the dangerous journey by boat to the ship which will take her from Bourbon to France, but its importance is still emotional and symbolic. As a woman, Indiana can do nothing; she is in the hands of the sailors. She can only sit silent and unyielding in the face of their taunts and the stormy sea, just as she survived her husband's abuse by mute defiance.

In a way, the plot is not particularly original. It consists of a series of conventional scenes, of seduction and betrayal, of flight and return, scenes set in drawing rooms, a bedroom and in nature, but what make them effective and new are the parallels and oppositions that Sand sets up between them, ones which reverse their normal significance as she gives conventional structures a twist of her own. The message of the novel is contained in the pattern of events, a pattern of repetition and inversion which successfully combines the traditional with the new as well as giving us the satisfaction of a finely ordered plot. The first half of the novel follows a well-trodden path: the worldly hero undertakes a parallel pair of seductions, first the maid then the mistress, but is suddenly brought short by the resistance of the second. The roles are now reversed, and it is the woman who pursues the man, not to seduce him but to ask for his protection. Twice she leaves the prison of her husband's house to go to his room and is twice dismissed. We anticipate a tragic conclusion but our expectations are again twice confounded. It seems at first that the novel will end with two deaths (those of Ralph and Indiana) though deaths freely chosen as the consummation of a life, not deaths from despair. But then the deaths themselves are reversed into a life lived happily ever after.

The first part of the novel acts as a kind of prologue which could stand alone as the conventional story of a maid's seduction leading to her suicide. Its importance, though, lies not so much in this story itself but in its anticipation of the rest of the book, the model it sets up for what is to come. For this first section also, and more importantly, prepares us for the seduction of Indiana, as Raymon is already switching his attentions from maid to mistress. This too seems to be aborted by Noun's death, as Indiana half understands the message it conveys although she does not yet know of Raymon's part in it, and she draws back from any further romantic involvement.

But Raymon persists and the narrative takes off again. The first scene of Part Two imitates in every way the opening scene of Part One, except that it is spring, not autumn, a possible anticipation of a happier outcome. The same three characters are present: Delmare, bored and restless, Indiana, brooding sadly over her needlework, and Ralph, impassively smoking his pipe. Again they are interrupted by news of Raymon's arrival, now as invited guest of Delmare instead of unwelcome interloper, as he resumes his seduction of Indiana, this time from a surer footing. It takes him much longer than it did with Noun, and he has to calculate each stage of his pursuit with great care. As with Noun, however, he succeeds eventually in gaining access to Indiana's room, where the dramatic and erotic bedroom scene of Part One is repeated, but with Indiana in the place of Noun. The moonlit night is damp and misty as it had been before, and Raymon is haunted by the ghostly memory of his previous mistress as he crosses the park on his way to Indiana's bedroom. When he gets there, Indiana plays up the similarity by inadvertently dressing as Noun had been dressed and then deliberately pretending that Noun's hair, which she had preserved, was her own, just as Raymon had confused the reflection and even the body of Noun with that of Indiana. But the two scenes, the two women, are not quite interchangeable. Noun delighted in succumbing to Raymon's caresses whereas Indiana after a moment of weakness refuses to give in. Then, as in a conventional melodrama, the scene is both times interrupted by the arrival of a third party, Indiana herself in Part One, and Ralph and Delmare in Part Two.

From this point on, the action goes into reverse. On both occasions, the challenge being over, Raymon ceases his pursuit, but as a response Noun drowns herself in typical Romantic fashion, while Indiana, untypically fearless, takes up the initiative. It is now she who seeks out Raymon in his room in Paris and he who is reluctant and brutally turns her away; 'Allons, madame, il est temps de vous retirer' (**222**). At this, Indiana's courage fails her since it was a courage still dependent on a man's love, and she reverts to the traditional woman's role, blindly wandering the streets in despair, instinctively drawn towards the river bank in a half-conscious imitation of the suicide of Noun. In a moment of utter hopelessness, she almost allows herself to be carried away by the water and is only saved by the unexpected appearance of

Ralph in his role of guardian angel sent to save the typical damsel in distress.

The high drama of this section is followed by a quiet interlude on the île Bourbon, to which Delmare, Indiana and Ralph now repair as a refuge in which Delmare may regain his fortune, and Indiana recover her spirit. It proves to be a false respite however, since Indiana is still obsessed by thoughts of France and her lover. Whereas Ralph gains a certain solace in the solitude of the mountains and in memories of his peaceful childhood there, Indiana hardly sees her beautiful surroundings but dreams only of Paris and Raymon: 'Elle vécut ainsi des semaines et des mois sous le ciel des tropiques, n'aimant, ne connaissant qu'une ombre, ne creusant qu'une chimère' (254). The reader too is reminded at intervals of what she has left behind and anticipates her return through the switches in narrative focus away from Bourbon back to France, where Raymon, in a passing moment of weakness and regret, writes to Indiana to summon her back to his side. The call, coinciding as it does with Delmare's worst act of violence against his wife when he pushes her over and stamps on her face with his boot, has immediate effect, and once more Indiana leaves her husband's house to join her lover.

This second flight is infinitely more difficult and testing than the first, and almost leads to her death. It is as though by abandoning the familiar framework of her marital home and the land of her childhood, she is left with no identity at all. On arriving in Bordeaux after her long sea journey, she finds the whole of France in turmoil as a result of the July Revolution, and at first she does not recognise the land she had left behind; thus her own disarray is paralleled and reinforced by that of the nation. She falls ill and is released from hospital two months later, alone, anonymous, a stranger to everyone 'sans argent, sans linge, sans effets' (291), having had her hair, symbol of her femininity, cropped in hospital. This is her first descent into the hell of non-being from which she recovers sufficiently to be able to find Raymon, now married and living in her own former home at le Lagny. Again it is she who goes to him (for the second time) in what was her bedroom, only to be finally dismissed not by Raymon who does not have the courage but by his cold, contemptuous wife (297).

Then follows her darkest moment as she finds herself in a cheap, shabby hotel room in Paris, overcome with despair, forgetting to eat or sleep and eventually losing consciousness. Again, as at Bordeaux, her environment mirrors her condition. She can sink no lower nor be more bereft: a hotel room, says the narrator, is a kind of terrible limbo through which crowds of anonymous people ceaselessly pass, leaving no trace of their passing, wretched travellers wandering the face of the earth, with only the desert of Paris outside, 'noir de boue et de pluie, bruyant, infect et rapide comme un torrent de fange' (299; see Schor's significant commentary in *1*, p. 104). For a woman, it is even worse, since a woman depends more on others for a sense of who she is. Here, on the point of death, Indiana is discovered by Ralph, her only remaining friend, her guardian angel come to save her again. He has reached her through a series of coincidences, beginning with her husband's death the very night she left home. But she has lost all will to live, any hope of happiness: 'elle tomba dans un état de langueur et d'apathie qui ressemblait à l'imbécillité' (304).

Gustave Planche, writing in the *Revue des Deux Mondes* of 30 November 1832, thought that the novel should have ended here, with the marriage of Raymon and the death of its heroine, and this would indeed have provided an effective, natural conclusion to this story of unrequited and forbidden love (362). James Vest sees the conclusion as totally unrealistic, straight out of a fairy tale or chivalric romance (p. 39); but Nancy Miller gives *Indiana* as an example of the way women authors may rewrite traditional, masculine, endings, refusing death or conventional marriage for their heroines and allowing them to resurrect into a different, freer *modus vivendi*: 'An ironic nineteenth-century female artist refuses the pathos and limits of the woman who embroiders her way through the plot of life' (p. 89). There can be no doubt that the idyllic, pastoral ending, with all its implausibilities, bears the strongest mark of Sand's own personal idealism.

But Indiana is not yet ready for her final redemption. Both she and Ralph need the long sea journey back to Bourbon, the land of their origins, to prepare for the climax. Indiana must finally rid herself of her infatuation with Raymon and see clearly the nobility and wisdom of Ralph: 'Enfin, à force de comparer ces deux hommes, tout vestige de son amour aveugle et fatal s'éteignit dans son âme' (309). Ralph needs to acquire the courage and self-confidence which will allow him at last to give voice to his most secret desires and so transcend his loneliness. The scene at Bernica not only removes us as far as possible from the verisimilitude of the rest of the book but also rewrites and takes further the idealist text of Bernardin de Saint-Pierre. For Bernardin's Virginie dies, unable to live in a world desecrated by sex, while the suicides of Indiana and Ralph are transformed into a spiritual consummation of their love which allows them to live on, purified of earthly longing. 'Alors Ralph prit sa fiancée dans ses bras, et l'emporta pour la précipiter avec lui dans le torrent...' (**330**). Two explanations are later given by Ralph for an implausible survival that is not reflected in the Laffont-Bompiani *Dictionnaire des Œuvres* entry: 'Elle se précipite dans le remous tourbillonnant d'une chute d'eau. L'énigmatique Ralph la suit dans son tragique destin' (III, 701). One is realistic (that he lost his way, so that the drop was of only a few feet), one supernatural (that an angel came down on a ray of moonlight and saved them), and it is the supernatural one that Ralph, and perhaps Sand, prefers. It is clearly a kind of *Liebestod manqué* which plays on conventional associations of love and death to lift the text onto the highest level of fantasy and myth.

In the conclusion, it seems that the action comes back down to earth; the couple are found to be living on in their remote sanctuary above the rocks, high up the valley of Bernica. Ralph occasionally visits the little port of Saint-Paul, and they discreetly intervene in social affairs by purchasing the freedom of sick or disabled slaves (**342**). But they are now seen from the outside, through the local inhabitants who have strangely contradictory views of Ralph's character, and through the first-person narrator, who has just made their acquaintance and is intrigued by their solitary life, so that the reader is allowed little access to their inner lives and the air of unreality is increased. Their existence appears timeless, paradisal; 'Tous nos jours se ressemblent; ils sont tous calmes et beaux; ils passent rapides et purs comme ceux de notre enfance' (**342**), and the final words of the text send us back to Bernardin de Saint-Pierre, not, as we have seen, to the partly socialised world of *Paul et Virginie* but to the utterly withdrawn natural dwelling-place of their own *Chaumière indienne*. From the Balzacian realism of the first part of the novel, with its faithful replication of the power structures of society, Sand has led us via a woman's rebellion first within the limits of convention, then outside them, to a conclusion whose Utopian idealism could not be further from the expectations set up by the beginning. She has transposed and inverted the traditional sequence of events in a quest romance in order to imbue them with her own feminist and socialist dreams.

(iv) Realism and symbolism

It is easy to see the narrative of *Indiana* in terms of its heroine's move from the real world of France in the years before and after the July Revolution to the idealised, mythical world of the île Bourbon. But such a reading, although accurate, is also misleadingly over-simplified; for it suggests that the two worlds are at opposite poles from each other, the one totally material and the other suggestive of a transcendental world beyond. In fact, Sand's creative symbolism infuses not only the remote valley of Bernica but also the actual places of le Lagny and Paris with a spiritual significance, a sense of the supernatural which implies to the reader that the world cannot be viewed exclusively through the eyes of the positivist materialist of the time. For although in her autobiography Sand explicitly dissociates herself from the fantastic effects of the *roman noir* (and indeed there are in *Indiana* none of the wild descriptions we associate with the gothic novels of Maturin or Ann Radcliffe), nevertheless the power of the novel resides as much in the symbolism, which hints at a supernatural both divine and demonic, as in the historical realism so praised by its contemporaries. As in Balzac's novels, particularly perhaps *La Peau de chagrin*, the two different aesthetic modes of which we have found evidence elsewhere in *Indiana* are not necessarily incompatible at the level of the writing. Within a literary text, realism (which can never, of course, give more than an illusion of reality) may combine with the symbolism of dreams so that the inner significance of that reality may be made more clear.

The opening scene of *Indiana* has often been seen as exemplary of the realist mode. The first sentence tells us where we are, at which season of the year, and what are the mundane occupations of its three characters: 'Par une soirée d'automne pluvieuse et fraîche, trois personnes rêveuses étaient gravement occupées, au fond d'un petit castel de la Brie, à regarder brûler les tisons du foyer et cheminer lentement l'aiguille de la pendule' (49). We are then given a full description of each person's appearance and something of his previous life. Other details are filled in, of the furnishings and decoration of the room, which clearly indicate both its age and its style: 'un vieux salon meublé dans le goût de Louis XV' (50). But gradually, as we read on, the scene becomes less real: it takes on the fixity, the timelessness of a dream. It is compared to a painting by Rembrandt (52), and our attention is drawn to the play of the firelight among the shadows which transforms the ordinary room into a place full of depth and mystery. The characters become like ghosts or like figures from a fairy tale, 'fixes et pétrifiés comme les héros d'un conte de fées' and the walls are now 'les murs d'une cité fantastique' which at any moment may crumble into dust (53).

Even when the figures move and speak, their behaviour seems strangely irrational: Delmare's sudden beating of the dog and Indiana's superstitious fear of an indefinable disaster to come. It is only with the entrance of the servant asking for a gun to make his evening rounds, and the arrival of the intruder, Raymon, that the spell is broken and the story is able to begin. We re-enter the real world, now clearly illuminated by the extra candle placed on the mantlepiece, a world where a man is wounded by a gunshot and is in need of practical care: 'On jeta un matelas sur quelques banquettes, et Indiana, aidée de ses femmes, s'occupa de panser la main malade tandis que sir Ralph [...] pratiqua une abondante saignée' (64). But what better way to prepare us for the story of a romantic, sensitive young woman, trapped in a brutal marriage, than to present her first like the traditional maiden, imprisoned without hope in a lonely, sombre castle by 'un sorcier qui les eût tenus sous le charme' (53), as Delmare is described. This apparently conventional tale is imbued from the beginning with a sense of another world, a feeling that not everything can be seen and understood in materialist terms, and this sense prepares us for the idealism of the end. Though urbane, the narrator has the imagination of his creator, entering into those moments when reality seems to open to reveal some ghostly mystery beneath.

As the novel advances, the picture we are given of the 'real' world becomes increasingly detailed and substantial, and we momentarily forget the dreamlike atmosphere of that first scene. Delmare owns a factory, whose industrial secrets

Raymon pretends to want to steal. Later, as a result of competition from his more powerful rivals, the factory goes bankrupt and Delmare is forced to take refuge in his old home on the île Bourbon in order to build up his fortune anew. The adopted father of Laure de Nangy is also an industrialist, richer and more successful than Delmare, and, as we have seen, it is to him and his ilk that the future belongs. All of this reflects the growing importance of industry and finance and the rise of the bourgeoisie throughout that period. The time at which part of the action takes place is specified more precisely as 'l'année Martignac' (128), named after the Minister of the Interior during the year 1828-1829, and is described in detail as a time of transition when the royalists attempted to make a deal with the liberals in order to avert the threat of a revolution. It is in this context that we should see the discussions between Raymon, Delmare and Ralph, who represent the different political stances of the time. Later we are given a rapid, graphic account of the effect of the July Revolution on the provincial town of Bordeaux, for Indiana disembarks just as it is breaking out: 'Une violente agitation bouleversait la ville; le préfet avait été presque massacré la veille; le peuple se soulevait de toutes parts; la garnison semblait s'apprêter à une lutte sanglante, et l'on ignorait encore l'issue de la révolution de Paris' (290). Passages like this give a strong sense of the social background within which Indiana's story unfolds, and at the same time, as we have seen, they go beyond realism to set up parallels between the turmoil of the time and the mental confusion of the main protagonist.

As well as such historical symbolism, Sand uses a kind of geographical symbolism, the symbolism of places, whereby the rooms of le Lagny and Paris, drawing rooms, ballrooms and bedrooms, become suggestive of enclosure and constraint as opposed to the open spaces of the île Bourbon, where Indiana can roam at will. This would imply that the real world of France is indeed as much part of the symbolic structure of the novel as the mountains and valleys of Bernica. It is noticeable how much of the symbolism is focused on the room as the space within which much of the action evolves. We have already seen how the drawing room of the opening scene becomes an eerie place full of shadows, which seems to transfix the characters and lock them into a world of dream. Equally, the anonymous hotel room takes on a symbolic significance as the hell in which one's very identity disappears, the inner circle of the damned, whereas Indiana's room on the île Bourbon is open to the outside world, gives on to the vast expanse of sky and mountain scenery in which Indiana can move freely and dream.

It is Indiana's bedroom at le Lagny that is the most rich in symbolic allusions. It is described by Stirling Haig as 'a sort of hermetic Venusberg' (p. 34). It clearly stands for Indiana herself and penetration of it suggests an attempt to possess her most intimate being. As readers, we may feel we are violating its sacred space ourselves as we first see it through the acquisitive eyes of Raymon as he is led there illicitly by Noun. It is hardly a real place at all. Although plausibly furnished with Indiana's simple possessions—her books, her needlework, her harp—its odd, circular shape evokes a perfect, magic space at the heart of the *château*; it resembles a womb, is expressive of Indiana's femininity, a femininity which is still virginal and untouched, summed up in 'ce petit lit à demi caché sous les rideaux de mousseline, ce lit blanc et pudique comme celui d'une vierge' **(101)**. The sense of a separate, charmed place is intensified by the many mirrors which increase our awareness of distance, but also of enclosure since it is always the same objects that are reflected back. The reflection, though, is vague and indeterminate, and in both bedroom scenes Raymon confuses the images of Noun and Indiana so that they almost become one. For him, the room is redolent of both, a feminine space in every sense, both virginal and sensual like the perfume of the flowers with which Noun has filled it. But on the wall opposite the bed, presiding over the room and excluding Raymon's erotic fancies, is a portrait of Ralph kept veiled when Indiana is absent, as though their intimacy is too private to be revealed to any strangers who may enter **(107-8)**. The fact that he is not seen as an intruder in this virginal place, coupled with his position there alongside the pastoral prints from *Paul et Virginie*, both looks back to their innocent childhood on the island together and forward to their spiritual union at the end.

Both bedroom scenes are preceded by a description of the park at le Lagny. It is a mysterious and frightening space which Raymon has to cross before gaining access to Indiana's room, an ordeal through which he must pass if he is to earn his reward. Each time, the trees are enveloped in a mist which rises from the river, and he almost loses the path as they become like ghostly presences which loom up in front of him to bar his way. The second time, after Noun's suicide by drowning, the atmosphere is particularly eerie as Raymon is haunted by his guilt and thinks he hears the sobbing of an abandoned child in the cries of the curlew and seems to see the phantom of Noun floating in the mist: 'contemplant d'un œil fixe et terrifié cette vague apparition qui restait là, flottante, incertaine, comme la brume de la rivière et le rayon tremblant de la lune' (186). This is a nightmare place, where perceptions are distorted and reality disappears.

The focus of Raymon's fears is the water where Noun drowned, and the reader too remembers the macabre picture of her dead body, half-caught in the reeds, floating slowly downstream in the dawn mist (119). In the first edition of the novel, the narrator developed the gothic potential of this description, concentrating on the drowned corpse's ghastly pallor and blue lips, only then to criticise its hyperboles. Sand removed the whole paragraph in the second edition but the original passage bears witness to the influence on her of the *roman noir* hovering beneath the text, even if this influence is finally denied. There is an explicit reminiscence of this scene later in the novel when Indiana, in despair, is tempted to imitate Noun and to allow herself to be carried away by the river water in Paris at dawn. The atmosphere is similar: outlines are blurred and misty as the white houses and grey sky are reflected in the murky water. Here she is saved by Ralph and the dog, Ophélia, whose name inevitably brings to mind another image of a drowned maiden, maltreated by a man, whose long hair is caught in the reeds. The dog is twice beaten in place of Indiana, first by Delmare and later by the sailors who are taking her to join the vessel bound for France. It then itself drowns, in a clear reminiscence of Noun's (and Ophelia's) death; its corpse floats a moment alongside the boat.

The name of the dog emphasises the importance of the leitmotif of suicide by drowning, and links maid and mistress, although the mistress's near-suicide at the end clearly reverses the implications of the motif. It takes the form of a deliberate plunge into a rushing torrent, not a passive floating away in the slowly flowing water of a river, and is miraculously transformed into a kind of spiritual survival beyond death. It is the second time that Indiana is said to be protected by a divine power which has her under its wing; the first time was when, out of the weakness of her fear, she suddenly found the strength to resist Raymon's brutal attempt at seduction: 'Indiana eut peur. Un bon ange étendit ses ailes sur cette âme chancelante et troublée; elle se réveilla et repoussa les attaques du vice égoïste et froid' **(221)**. In this way, the reality of mortal striving is doubled by a supernatural world in which forces of good and evil do battle for human souls and finally open to them the gates of Paradise.

In this novel, it is of course the île Bourbon that takes the place of Paradise. Yet, just as the mundane reality of le Lagny and Paris has a supernatural dimension, so Bourbon, in spite of the subsequent disclaimer—'Pourtant je ne pus me défendre [...] de commettre peut-être quelques erreurs de géographie sur leur oasis finale. Je n'y tenais guère' (*Vie*, p. 167)—, is also a real place, evoked through detailed and accurate descriptions of its geography, its bird and plant life. On its shores is the port of Saint-Paul, the essential line of communication between the island and the outside world, inhabited by the most ordinary of men, prejudiced and prone to gossip. Even the valley of Bernica actually existed and its different geological features were described to Sand by her friend Jules Néraud, as she was anxious to get the details right. Yet it is strangely impenetrable, something like the Eldorado of Voltaire's *Candide*, hidden behind massive walls of rock in bizarre and apparently magical formations; 'Les esprits de l'air et du feu présidèrent sans doute à cette diabolique opération; [...] eux seuls ont pu entasser ces blocs effrayants, remuer ces masses gigantesques, jouer avec les monts comme avec des grains de sable [...]' **(332)**. These rocks seem to be covered in curious inscriptions, apparently by an immortal hand, to which the passer-by tries in vain to attach a meaning. Miller suggests an allusion here to the unreadability of the world and, more particularly, the enigmatic conclusion to this text: 'the female landscape is [...] the iconography of a desire for a revision of story, and in particular a revision of closure' (pp. 86-87). Once again, the realist, positivist view falls short; even if Sand did not quite intend so specific a reference, the presence of these strange, giant stones is oddly gratuitous.

The novel comes to a climax in the final scene at Bernica before the epilogue, as Indiana and Ralph prepare to plunge headlong into the rushing waters of the cataract. It is here too that the idealist message and symbolic writing both reach their peak. Everything comes together to create a setting fit for the rite of passage they are undertaking, a marriage as well as a death. The mountains are bathed in soft moonlight, the air is filled with the perfume of flowers, the birds are still and the only sound is the falling water echoing against the banks. Dressed in white, glowing in the light of the moon, with orange blossom in her hair, Indiana is like a virgin bride, far from the sad, ailing girl of the beginning, and Ralph too is transfigured by the final, full expression of his love, seeming to Indiana sublime and radiant, like a god. They are both in a state of heightened ecstasy and spiritual intoxication. Their love is consummated by their first kiss, the seal of their union on earth and in heaven, as Ralph takes his fiancée in his arms and leads her to the edge of the precipice (330). The suspension points with which this part of the text ends allow the reader to linger in their world of dream, to imagine a conclusion too exalted to be put into words, before coming back to reality at the beginning of the next chapter with the arrival of the first-person narrator at Saint-Paul 'au mois de janvier dernier'. Time has started up again, the union of Ralph and Indiana becomes earthbound, subject to the laws of human psychology. As Ralph says, 'ce ne fut pas en un jour que je pus m'affermir dans l'espoir de plaire et d'être aimé' (341). Their transcendent experience on the mountainside has not played them false, however, and the inference is that they will live happily ever after in true fairytale style. The demons of society and false love have been vanquished and the ideal world is truly theirs.

Conclusion

For Kristina Wingård Vareille, the critical interest of *Indiana* resides mainly in its composite nature, as the different literary codes within which it works all enter into conflict with one another: *Indiana* 'appartient à ces œuvres bâtardes, génériquement parlant, dans lesquelles les conflits des codes ou des registres est en grande partie constitutif de leur portée critique' (p. 61). Idealism is set against realism, the social places limits on the personal, subjective and objective views alternate, and no one way of looking at the world remains unquestioned. To these opposing tendencies can be added the inconsistencies

which result from the twists Sand gives to conventional forms
in order to make them express her own personal convictions.
The possibility of there being several alternative readings of
Indiana, in particular the didactic as against the mimetic, is
strengthened by Sand's own writings on her novel, the
prefaces of 1832 and 1842, the 'Notice' of 1852, the twelfth
Lettre d'un voyageur addressed to Nisard (1836), and certain
passages of her autobiography, *Histoire de ma vie* (1847-1854),
each of which emphasises different aspects of the work. The
preface of 1832 is itself somewhat confused. Written in the
voice of the male narrator, it is modest but also defensive. The
novel is described first as a 'une œuvre sans importance' (37)
and its author as a 'simple diseur, chargé de vous amuser et
non de vous instruire' (38). Any message the text may appear to
put forward should be attributed to the blatant faults of the
society it is depicting realistically and objectively: 'l'écrivain
n'est qu'un miroir qui les reflète' (37), an argument already
more ironically rehearsed by the narrator of *Le Rouge et le
Noir* (Book II, Chapter 19). All we find in the novel is simply 'la
moralité qui sort des faits' (although of course the reader
knows it is the author who has decided what that morality
should be, and has fixed the facts accordingly). Sand's hidden
polemical purpose, however, becomes more obvious later in
the preface: 'Peut-être que tout l'art du conteur consiste à
intéresser à leur propre histoire les coupables qu'il veut
ramener, les malheureux qu'il veut guérir' (41), as the
vocabulary of guilt and correction used here is strongly
suggestive of a particular moral view.

In the 'Lettre à M. Nisard', written in reponse to an 1836
article by the critic Désiré Nisard in the *Revue de Paris*, Sand,
speaking clearly now as author of *Indiana* rather than
narrator, defends herself more overtly against charges of
immorality, in particular the charge that adulterous affairs are
condoned in several of her novels. She begins by denying
(rightly) than any adultery is committed in Indiana (p. 936), and
points out that the figure of the lover is even more antipathetic
than the husband. By then comparing her novels to comedies,
however, and describing them as an 'école de mœurs' (p. 939),
she does accept that she has a moral intention although she
insists that she is not attacking social institutions like marriage,
but rather certain practices within those institutions: 'J'ai eu
tort aussi de dire souvent le *mariage* au lieu des *personnes*

mariées'(p. 939). She insists that she has a profound veneration for the ideal of marriage itself, an ideal of tenderness, fidelity and of the sanctity of the family as opposed to 'l'espèce de contrat honteux et de despotisme stupide qu'a engendrés l'infâme décrépitude du monde' (p. 941). By using such violent language, she makes plain the strength of personal feeling that lay behind her creation of figures like Delmare, and when she attacks the double standard of a society which condones adultery in a husband but not a wife she is no doubt thinking more of her own experience with the unfaithful Casimir than of her heroine, who is never sexually betrayed by Delmare. Here, quite clearly, the voice of the woman takes over from the detached view of the realist author.

In the 1842 preface to a new edition of the novel, she is even more self-confident and outspoken, as this period coincides with her more obviously socialist and feminist texts. While stressing her immaturity and naivety at the time of writing *Indiana*, she explicitly defines the inspiration behind the work as 'le sentiment non raisonné, il est vrai, mais profond et légitime, de l'injustice et de la barbarie des lois qui régissent encore l'existence de la femme dans le mariage, dans la famille et la société' (46-47). What had been a simple feeling of outrage has now become a reasoned principle, and she makes deliberate use of this second preface to a work she had written ten years earlier unambiguously to articulate her present hatred of the inequalities of the married state. Indeed, here she is probably exaggerating her original moral intention in accordance with the views of the disillusioned adult she has now become, for this retrospective, polemical reading is as overly simplistic as the earlier one which stressed the objective realism of the work. *Indiana* is about many things besides the position of women in marriage. It is about altruism and equality for all the silenced and dispossessed. It also depicts a young woman's natural romanticism, her personal search for fulfilment, and her deluded infatuation with a seductive Don Juan, all of which are only partly explicable by her marital situation. Through the narrator's generalisations, too, many of Indiana's characteristics are presented as common to all women, whether married or not, and as a result, the interest of the novel is psychological as well as moral and social. And, as we have seen, its picture of French society between 1827 and 1832, in the provinces, in Paris and on the île Bourbon, is detailed and comprehensive, including references to politics, industrialisation and colonisation which go far beyond Indiana's loveless marriage. None of this is mentioned in the 1842 preface.

Later on, the emphasis shifts again, and in her autobiography Sand gives a more balanced and subtle view of her literary aims, stressing the combination of realism and idealism in all her works, 'l'idéalisation du sentiment [...] dans un cadre de réalité assez sensible pour le faire ressortir' (*Vie*, p. 161). She had been struck, she says, by the originality of Balzac's realist novels and thought of him as 'un maître à étudier' (p. 154) as opposed to other, more extravagant, masters: 'À cette époque on faisait les choses les plus étranges en littérature' (p. 159). But she accepts too that at the origin of the writing of *Indiana* was 'un sentiment bien net et bien ardent, l'horreur de l'esclavage brutal et bête' (p. 164), while maintaining that the characters who embody this polemical purpose are placed within the context of real life. They are symbolic figures, whose significance is made clear by the idealism of the denouement; for this she does not apologise, but they can only be made convincing by the social and historical realism of the setting and the other characters. Neither here nor anywhere else does she have any intention of self-portraiture as a female: 'je ne me suis jamais mise en scène sous des traits féminins. [...] Mon *moi*, me revenant face à face, m'eût toujours refroidie' (p. 160).

Another striking element of Sand's writings on *Indiana*, in particular the last, brief 'Notice' of 1852, is the violent attack on the many critics who, she says, have distorted her work in an attempt to make it conform to their own moral prejudices, for example by insisting on seeing *Indiana* simply as 'un plaidoyer bien prémédité contre le mariage' (35). For them, the concern of a novel is not to render the concrete complexity of individual lives but to promote a particular ideology which they then brand as immoral and subversive in an all-out attack on the freedom of literary works. Sand is arguing here for an open and flexible reading, which does not try to impose a false unity but is sympathetic to a multiplicity of interpretations and sensitive to a novel's different tones. And surely this is the right way to read *Indiana*; it is as mistaken to try to classify the novel within one clear literary mode or authorial intention as it is to deny the complexity of its young, androgynous author.

Mauprat

In the five years between the publication of *Indiana* in 1832 and the serialization of *Mauprat* in April and May 1837, Sand produced seven novels, more than one a year, partly because this had become her way of earning a living but also as a means of self-expression and debate. These novels take further the discussion initiated in *Indiana* of the relations between men and women both inside and outside marriage, and explore in greater depth a woman's attitude to her sexuality (see *Lélia* in particular). Sand experiments with various literary forms, using different situations and narrative perspectives in order to approach the issue from different angles, and in so doing comes closer to finding her own voice. The focus is still largely on the private and personal, as in *Indiana*. In *Simon* (1836), however, and most obviously in *Mauprat*, her concerns become more overtly social and political as well as moral, a tendency already evident in her non-fictional writings of this period (*Lettres d'un voyageur*, 1834-1836; *Lettres à Marcie*, 1837).

It is generally agreed that these new concerns were at least partly the result of her acquaintanceship in 1835-1836 with two contemporary thinkers, Félicité de Lamennais and Pierre Leroux, and also of her passionate affair with the lawyer and political activist Michel de Bourges, but she was also growing in confidence and was no longer afraid to use her novels as propaganda for her own views on society. Her popularity as writer and literary personality was assured. Thus, although *Mauprat* (like *Indiana*) owes something to various traditional fictional genres—the Gothic novel, chivalric romance, the *Bildungsroman*, detective fiction, the historical novel—the finished product is an original and successful creation which goes beyond all these and expresses Sand's views on history and social progress as well as on the situation of women in marriage. The Gothic is transformed into the Utopian in what Jean-Pierre Lacassagne calls 'une magistrale *déconstruction* du genre' (**21**); the chivalric romance is both a novel of education and a passionate battle for sexual control. All these influences, instead of remaining in contradiction (as they do to some extent in *Indiana*), are resolved into a convincing and morally significant whole. For example, the two figures of Indiana and Noun, doubles and opposites, have become one central heroine, Edmée, the narrative perspective and plot now have a single focus, Bernard's transformation, and the message borne by the happy ending is clear, if impossibly idealistic.

The novel was written in two separate stages, begun in 1835, then abandoned until the winter of 1836-1837, and although there is some dispute as to the content of the initial draft, this would suggest that Sand's intentions changed as the first version was abandoned, to be picked up again only a year and a half later. During this interim time, as well as pursuing her new socialist concerns, Sand was engaged in lengthy legal proceedings to finalise her separation from her husband, and conducting an increasingly stormy affair with the tyrannical de Bourges, who was acting as her lawyer. Although *Mauprat* seems to owe less to events of her own life than does *Indiana*, there is no doubt that these personal experiences left their mark, encouraging her to think further about woman's nature and situation in society. Bernard's trial in La Châtre and Bourges reflects Sand's own entanglement with the law in the same two towns, as she also had to face the court twice in defence of her right to a separation. More importantly, however, the novel as a whole expresses Sand's continuing preoccupation with the marriage relationship, its problems and any possible solutions. As in the 'Lettre à M. Nisard' of 1836, she was keen to make clear that her quarrel was not with the institution of marriage itself but with contemporary practice and social mores. As she says in the 'Notice' of 1851: 'plus je venais de voir combien il est pénible et douloureux d'avoir à rompre de tels liens, plus je sentais que ce qui manque au mariage, ce sont des éléments de bonheur et d'équité d'un ordre trop élevé pour que la société actuelle s'en préoccupe' (33). In this way, she links the question of equality in marriage to her socialist concerns, to the wider issue of political equality within society, demonstrating also in the novel how important the right kind of education is to the achieving of both. The feminism of her earlier works is allied to her new-found socialism and interest in education, showing convincingly how the range of her thinking has broadened.

For example, she introduces a new literary figure, Patience, the visionary peasant, seen as a parallel to Edmée; each represents a weaker, oppressed section of society—women and peasants—who move from the margins of power to the centre. Both are largely self-educated (as was Sand herself), implying a criticism of contemporary educational methods, and both become educators and guides, of Bernard, the hero, and also in the small world in which they live. In order to carry through this change of roles, Sand exploits and revises some previous narratives which had dealt with a similar theme and are clearly at the origin of her novel. Yvette Bozon-Scalzitti, in her article, makes much of the resemblances between *Mauprat* and Madame le Prince de Beaumont's *La Belle et la Bête* (1775), in which a hideous monster is regenerated by the love of a woman; she emphasises the role reversal effected by Sand, whereby Beauty is always in control of the Beast. Similarly, the male figure of Pygmalion, legendary king, through whose love a statue is brought to life, becomes the female aristocrat, Edmée, and the humble peasant, Patience, who work together to transform a brutalised 'enfant sauvage' (188; 425) into a civilised and sensitive potential husband.

The most important text, however, with which Sand enters into debate is *Émile*, Rousseau's narrative of an exemplary education, published in 1762; and again the woman replaces the man as the primary educator. Edmée clearly follows Rousseau in the emphasis she gives to the moral and social aspects of an education rather than the academic:

> Edmée avait une sorte de direction occulte sur mes études; elle voulut que l'on ne m'enseignât pas le latin, assurant qu'il était trop tard pour consacrer plusieurs années à une science de luxe, et que l'important était de former mon cœur et ma raison avec des idées, au lieu d'orner mon esprit avec des mots. (203)

She also wishes to conceal from Bernard the part she plays in directing his development, so that he is encouraged to learn for himself: 'Mais en ceci elle était imbue de l'*Émile*, et mettait en pratique les idées systématiques de son cher philosophe' (204). For the misogynist Rousseau, however, these educational principles were relevant only to the education of a man, who was to be formed for public life; women should be trained merely for domesticity and the home. Here, though, it is clear that Edmée's (self-) education in its freedom from constraint was similar to that suggested for Émile. She has taught herself to reflect on wide social and moral issues and has become a kind of *femme philosophe* rather than the good wife and mother Rousseau is thinking of in his creation of Sophie for Émile. Yet she seems unaware of the differences between her and Rousseau and apparently agrees with his patronizing views on women: 'Edmée ne savait rien objecter quand Rousseau avait prononcé; elle aimait à reconnaître avec lui que le plus grand charme d'une femme est dans l'attention intelligente et modeste qu'elle donne aux discours graves' (222-3; we wonder whether these are also the views of Sand). As we shall see later, Patience too is an enthusiastic follower of Rousseau, particularly of his religious credo, *Profession de foi d'un vicaire savoyard*, but also of his belief in the importance of the right education: 'Je m'imagine que, de père en fils, les éducations vont se perfectionnant' (158).

Mauprat appears, then, primarily to be a novel of education, describing step by step the stages through which Bernard must pass in order to become civilised and enlightened, and worthy of an ideal marriage with the woman he loves. But his progress is also seen (by his friend Arthur) as a series of tests similar to those undergone by a medieval knight in pursuit of his lady: 'tu es un noble preux, condamné par ta dame à de rudes épreuves' (249). So the novel is also a love story, although a close examination of the way in which the love is presented reveals it to be less the straightforward chivalric romance that Arthur describes than a violent duel for power between two equally strong and passionate lovers, each trying to dominate and force the other to submit. Bernard and Edmée are not simple opposites like Beauty and the Beast, teacher and pupil, chaste lady and obedient suitor; they both have something of the androgyne about them (like Indiana and Ralph, and Sand herself), for Bernard is partly feminised by his forced dependency and Edmée is described by him as 'un jeune homme de mon âge, beau comme un séraphin' (197). They are also from the same family—'Sa tante à la mode de Bretagne' (409)—and have inherited a similar temperament, presented at times as a kind of fatality. Both were brought up exclusively by men, having lost their mothers at the same early age. They are cousins, like brother and sister, with the same strong will, ardent nature and aggressive instincts, the same 'fierté souveraine, une volonté de fer, un profond mépris pour la vie' (187), as Edmée tells the abbé Aubert. Indeed, both the strengths

and the weaknesses of the two cousins are similar: 'Bernard
seul me semble aussi fier, aussi colère, aussi hardi que moi et
aussi faible que moi; car il pleure comme un enfant quand je
l'irrite, et voilà que je pleure aussi en songeant à lui' (427). The
battle between them is closely linked to the battle between the
two sides of the Mauprat family—Coupe-jarret and Casse-
tête—as to which side will produce the heir; the title *Mauprat*
could refer to either one, to both, or to the family as a whole. It
is only through their marriage at the end of the book that the
conflict between them and within each one can be resolved.

So a pattern of opposites is set up between which the hero
and heroine are caught, and which to some extent goes against
the linear structure of a novel of education: good and evil,
civilization and nature, Sainte-Sévère and la Roche-Mauprat,
education and fatality. The contrasts are clear within Bernard,
but Edmée too, as well as being an educator and an ideal Muse,
is a woman in love who must fight to control her passionate,
instinctive desires and whose behaviour as a result is not
always consistent and logical. Since their story is narrated by
Bernard, who never fully understands his cousin, her conflict
remains at the margins of the text, her story is never fully told.
Nonetheless it is powerful enough to disrupt the even line of
Bernard's development 'de loup en homme' (38), so that he
several times feels that any progress is illusory and he has
returned to where he started: 'je me retrouvai précisément
dans les mêmes termes avec elle qu'au moment où j'étais tombé
malade' (208), and 'je me trouvais au même point que le jour de
son entretien avec l'abbé' (239). The love story seems almost to
take over from the novel of education, subverting it, pushing it
into second place as the realism of the characters'
psychological battles tempers the idealism of the conclusion. In
the end, though, they work together, and the lesson of the text
is filled out and made more convincing by the sympathy
engendered for the main characters as they struggle with effort
and difficulty towards their reward.

The final message is a relative one. Rousseau's optimism is
not always fully borne out by experience. Where an individual
is concerned, the question Bernard poses at the beginning of the
text: 'Y a-t-il en nous des penchants invincibles, et l'éducation
peut-elle les modifier seulement ou les détruire?' (53) cannot be
fully answered: 'l'homme ne naît pas méchant; il ne naît pas
bon non plus, comme l'entend Jean-Jacques Rousseau' (433).

There is no contradiction here, however, only a sense of moderation and compromise more in keeping with our experience of life than are the polarised opposites of *Indiana*.

(ii) Education

Mauprat as a novel of education traces Bernard's development through three different stages in three distinct locations: intellectual at Sainte-Sévère, social in Paris, and moral in America under the guidance of his new friend, Arthur. Although he was brought up by his widowed mother for the first seven years of his life until her death, these origins are barely mentioned, and the place from which Bernard comes, his starting point, is established beyond doubt as the sinister castle of la Roche-Mauprat, enclosed in a deep ravine and overshadowed by huge trees, to which he was brought by his grandfather at the age of seven after a horrific ride through the night. The novel opens with a description of la Roche-Mauprat's situation on the border between two regions, la Marche and le Berry, belonging to neither, in a kind of sombre enclave left over from the past and haunted by evil spirits. The young first narrator says he is always reminded, when he passes near, of the terrifying stories of his childhood, of Dick Turpin and Bluebeard or of 'les légendes surannées de l'Ogre et de Croquemitaine' (36). When Bernard takes over the narration, these fancies are given a terrible reality as the mode of living of Tristan, Bernard's grandfather, and his eight sons during the narrator's childhood is described in detail. It was a totally masculine society, 'le dernier débris [...] de cette race de petits tyrans féodaux' (45), which had been left behind by the advances of civilization, and still believed in the primitive, brutal manners of the Middle Ages. Its inhabitants had broken with all civil law, imposed slavery by force on the local peasantry and acquired a well-deserved reputation for injustice and violence. Old Mauprat is compared to a wild boar, a lynx and a fox (50), but at least he maintained a semblance of order and discipline, however backward-looking, within the castle. After his death, la Roche-Mauprat becomes still more isolated, the eight sons behaving with increased cowardice and lawlessness towards the local people, who

begin to resent their dominance. The scene is set for the
catastrophe, the horrific night when Edmée is lost in the forest
and taken prisoner by the brothers, coincidentally at the same
time as the local militia finally decides to impose order on the
criminals of la Roche-Mauprat, attacks the castle and kills
most of its inhabitants. The imagery is both Gothic and satanic,
not unlike that of Emily Brontë's *Wuthering Heights* (Thomson,
pp. 80-89). The castle is battered by a howling wind and
pouring rain, then lit up by the flickering flames of torches
before being set on fire. Bernard and Edmée (trapped orphan
and maiden in distress), who have been left alone during the
attack, make a pact of fidelity which is to play a very important
role in their love story, and escape hand in hand from the castle
by an underground passage, their ears assaulted by the
incessant sound of gunfire from the continuing battle.

The scene provides a fittingly dramatic setting for Bernard's
passage from the hell of la Roche-Mauprat into the paradise of
Sainte-Sévère, Edmée's home, which he reaches at dawn. But
he has lived at la Roche-Mauprat for ten years and has
necessarily been marked by his experiences there, as well as by
the characteristics inherited from his cursed family. Bernard as
narrator admits that even during his early years with his
mother, 'j'étais déjà violent, mais d'une violence sombre et
concentrée, aveugle et brutal dans la colère, méfiant jusqu'à la
poltronnerie à l'approche du danger, hardi jusqu'à la folie
quand j'étais aux prises avec lui' (53). He gives as an example
of his arrogance and violent tendencies the incident where he
accidentally killed Patience's pet owl in an act of revenge on the
'sorcier' that hits the wrong target (70-74). But he is also keen
to clear himself of the worst crimes committed by his uncles,
whom he feared and hated so intensely that he also hated what
they did. 'Peut-être n'avais-je en moi aucune force pour la
vertu, mais j'en avais heureusement pour la haine' (55), and
again: 'tout ce que je sais, c'est que j'eprouvais un affreux
malaise en présence de ces actions iniques' (57). He sums
himself up at the end of the chapter; 'Du reste, j'avais le
caractère aussi mal fait que mes compagnons; et, si mon cœur
valait mieux, mes manières n'étaient pas moins arrogantes ni
mes plaisanteries de meilleur goût' (58). Such is his character,
apparently as boorish as his uncles', but perhaps not completely
degenerate since he is still a child when he is suddenly removed
from the home of his early years and introduced into a paradise

of civilisation, tolerance and love. The first sign of this is the
tender devotion with which Edmée and her father greet each
other after the anguish of her disappearance the preceding
night. As he watches, Bernard feels a mixture of incredulity and
intense jealousy which shows how far he has to go before being
worthy of a place in this branch of his family.

The chevalier Hubert de Mauprat, Edmée's father,
represents the other side of the Mauprat clan and is a quite
different kind of aristocrat, who has a strong pride in his rank
and name but who has accepted the new values of tolerance
and respect between the classes preached by the
Enlightenment. He welcomes Bernard whole-heartedly into
the family out of his need for a son and heir, but also out of true
Christian charity, and promises to rebuild for him the castle of
la Roche-Mauprat and repay the family's debts. 'Vous êtes
orphelin, et je n'ai pas de fils. Voulez-vous m'accepter pour
votre père?' (127). Thus a pact is set up between them, like the
pact formed with Edmée in the underground passage; but
Bernard is even more uncouth than either Hubert or Edmée
had realised, and for a long time feels imprisoned and out of
place in the refined atmosphere of Sainte-Sévère. For the first
month he does not change at all; he is like a lion, a bear, a
badger, a wolf; he does not understand Hubert's generosity
and refuses any education. He prowls around the castle,
drinking too much, talking too loud, and constantly spying on
Edmée and her fiancé with lustful, jealous eyes.

The turning point comes as a result of two crucial
conversations, one between Bernard in the park and Edmée
protected behind the walls of the chapel, and the other, the
following night, between Edmée and the abbé Aubert, which is
overheard by Bernard. In the first of these, Edmée expresses
her affection to Bernard but swears that she will have nothing
to do with him unless he changes from a savage to a civilised
man and accepts an education. In the second, Edmée describes
to Aubert her fear of him and yet declares her loyalty to their
pact and her fidelity until death: 'j'irai jusqu'au jour de mes
noces, et, si Bernard m'est trop odieux, je me tuerai après le
bal' (192). These two scenes are separated by a decisive moonlit
walk in the park, when for the first time Bernard opens himself
to the beauty of nature, here seen as divinely redemptive not
satanic, and by a revealing conversation with Patience, now his
friend, who gives him a lesson about equality in society and

encourages him with his certainty that Edmée does not love her fiancé. The critical role of these moments is made clear: 'jusque-là, je n'avais pas cessé d'être l'homme de la Roche-Mauprat' (171), followed by: 'je n'étais déjà plus l'homme de la veille' (180). Bernard has realised that his physical lust for Edmée will not earn him what he wants, and he is also impressed and reassured by Edmée's sense of honour, which will not allow her to go back on her oath. He now sees Edmée not as a sexual creature, a potential mistress, but as a young man, friend and advisor (197); his love for her is purified and becomes a kind of heavenly devotion rather than possessive desire. The next morning he asks the abbé Aubert for lessons: we are exactly halfway through the book and his education is about to begin.

He turns out to be an amazingly quick learner. From a state of almost total illiteracy, 'au bout d'un mois je m'exprimais avec facilité et j'écrivais purement' (203), although as narrator he modestly ascribes this rapid progress to his willpower rather than to his intelligence. It is at this point that Edmée applies to him the educational principles she has learnt from her master, Rousseau, reading and discussing with him her favourite, mainly eighteenth-century authors—Condillac, Fénelon, Bernardin de Saint-Pierre, Rousseau, Montaigne and Montesquieu—in order to impress upon bim the humane, civilised values of the Enlightenment. The strain he puts himself under causes him to fall ill, another essential rite of passage which results in his shedding his old self and emerging back into health some weeks later. This transformation is confirmed by Edmée's passing her ring on his finger at the height of his delirium as a token of her fidelity. The rapidity of his progress, however, convinces him of his superiority and produces in him a terrible vanity which the narrator suspects is an innate vice which it will be another essential aim of his education to eradicate: 'Il est à croire que nous portons en nous, dès nos premiers ans, le germe des vertus et des vices que l'action de la vie extérieure féconde avec le temps' (210). He begins to quarrel with his uncle, arrogantly disagreeing with his old-fashioned views and driving him into a rage of frustration. He has learnt to read and to think, but his manners are as yet anything but civilised.

The next stage of his education, when he is brought to Paris by the family, is intended to correct this vice by introducing him

to a wider circle of acquaintances against which he may
measure himself, but unfortunately it has the opposite effect.
He observes the society around him, compares his own newly-
awakened vitality, energy and curiosity with their world-
weariness and jaded intelligence, and is further convinced of
his superiority. As narrator, he laments his presumption but
seems to agree with his self-assessment: 'J'étais jeune et bien
constitué, condition première peut-être de la santé du cerveau;
mes études n'étaient pas étendues, mais elles étaient solides; on
m'avait servi des aliments sains et d'une digestion facile' (220).
Like Voltaire's Ingénu, he combines the qualities of the savage
with those of the educated man to achieve a kind of balance,
but in him it is vitiated by his false vanity in affecting the
persona of the unworldly *philosophe* (Rousseau, for example),
refusing to dress smartly or powder his hair and insisting on
wearing clumsy, country boots. Unfortunately, his arrogance
also leads him to expect more commitment from Edmée, and
this, combined with his jealousy of fiancé Adhémar de la
Marche, leads to a violent scene in which he refuses to release
her from her vow of fidelity and reverts to being the
intemperate, uncontrollable beast of la Roche-Mauprat: 'Je ne
comprends rien, sinon que je vous aime avec fureur et que je
déchirerai avec mes ongles le cœur de celui qui osera vous
disputer à moi' (236). He ends his furious speech by swearing to
kill her if she marries someone else: 'j'ai juré par le nom de
Mauprat' (236). She makes clear his regression to his origins in
the dark side of the family by responding coldly: 'De Mauprat
coupe-jarret!' (237). He had even known the danger: 'Edmée!
Edmée! ne jouez pas avec le lion endormi, ne rallumez pas le
feu qui couve sous la cendre' (232), but is unable to avoid it. His
education seems to have come to naught, and he is back where
he began.

    And yet, in theory, he was convinced of the importance of
tolerance and respect for other people. Paris at that time was
full of talk of the American War of Independence then being
waged across the ocean, and the new values of equality and
freedom, originally promoted by the French *philosophes*, had
infiltrated the highest levels of society at least as talking-
points. Nourished by his reading at Sainte-Sévère, Bernard's
enthusiasm is quickly fired, and he espouses the ideals of the
American revolutionaries, although, as we have seen, he is
incapable of applying them to his own situation. It is perhaps

natural that, rejected at this point by Edmée and ashamed of his moment of violence with her, he should seek to prove the reality of his transformation by setting off to fight with the Americans against their colonial oppressors. France had sided with the rebels and was sending a fleet of ships to bring them aid. Twenty-four hours after his quarrel with Edmée, Bernard writes her a note of apology, setting her free from her vow of fidelity, and leaves secretly in the middle of the night to join the French army in its expedition across the Atlantic. His education is about to enter its third phase; his mind is now formed, he has learnt of the egoism and frivolity of the world, but has yet to attain self-knowledge and self-control.

His intention was to prove himself through glorious military exploits, like the knights of old, but although he is quickly a successful soldier, this is not what the narrative is concerned with. This is a *Bildungsroman* written by a woman who is less interested in the merits of public action than eager to promote the personal values of truth to oneself and consideration of others. In this pursuit, success on the battlefield is irrelevant. So this section of the novel concentrates instead on Bernard's new-found friendship with the exemplary figure of Arthur, who is a kind of masculine role model and the first young man of his age he has known. He is a young American botanist, described as 'pur comme un ange, désintéressé comme un stoïque, patient comme un savant, et avec cela enjoué et affectueux' (**244**), and again as 'l'envoyé du ciel; sans lui je fusse redevenu peut-être, sinon le coupe-jarret de la Roche-Mauprat, du moins le sauvage de la Varenne' (**245**).

Arthur introduces Bernard to the wonder and variety of Nature, no longer as a reflection of heaven or hell, but for itself. At the same time, he teaches him to analyse himself and govern his violent impulses, and in this way crucially furthers his education: 'On ne change pas l'essence de son être, mais on dirige vers le bien ses facultés diverses; on arrive presque à utiliser ses défauts; c'est au reste le grand secret et le grand problème de l'éducation' (**246**). He helps Bernard to understand Edmée's strange behaviour, reassures him of what he believes to be her continuing love, and encourages him to persevere in his expiation of his faults through exile and suffering. He admires what he sees as Edmée's strength of mind, which elevates her 'au-dessus de la faiblesse et de l'inertie de son sexe' (**251**) and makes her worthy of being truly loved. Here

Arthur is probably acting as a mouthpiece for Sand as he sets Edmée up as an ideal female figure, strong and patient, fitting object of a man's devotion rather than a creature to be dominated and possessed, and then cast aside.

Six years pass (in twenty-two pages); the war is over and Bernard is ready to return to France and to Edmée: 'Un immense changement s'était opéré en moi dans le cours de six années. J'étais un homme à peu près semblable aux autres; les instincts étaient parvenus à s'équilibrer presque avec les affections et les impressions avec le raisonnement' (280). His transformation has been accomplished and his education is complete, though the expressions 'à peu près' and 'presque' may arouse some disquiet. Edmée seems satisfied, but is still unwilling to allow him his reward in spite of her father's desire for their marriage, which would finally give him a son and heir. So the happy ending is deferred and Bernard must undergo a final test.

As a sign that the story is not over, that evil has not been entirely vanquished either within Bernard or in the world around him, the action moves back to the castle of la Roche-Mauprat, which Bernard needs to visit to supervise its reconstruction. The ghosts of his past return to haunt him: 'Je crus voir passer, en cet instant, les spectres de tous les Mauprat avec leurs mains sanglantes et leurs yeux hébétés par le vin' (287). We are back in the melodramatic world of the opening section of the novel, with its ruined castle, hidden passages, secret rendezvous and false monks. The atmosphere of the novel changes: Edmée seems vulnerable, pale and thin, her father is ill, and it is now they who need Bernard to look after them. He is left alone to battle against the forces of evil represented by Jean and Antoine de Mauprat, sole survivors of the original massacre, and he almost succumbs to them and to the Mauprat blood within him: 'le volcan se ralluma dans mon sein' (331). As Edmée contines to keep him at arm's length, he feels increasingly frustrated, as though there are two men inside him, the old and the new: 'il faut bien espérer que le brigand succombera; mais il se défend pied à pied' (333).

The conflict is terrible; Bernard tries desperately to cling on to his new, civilised self, but the beast of the past, in the form of his almost uncontrollable physical desire for Edmée, will not be restrained. We are near the catastrophic climax of the novel, when Edmée is shot during a hunt and Bernard is accused of attempting to kill her. Although we know that he is innocent, he could almost have been guilty. His nerves were stretched to breaking point by the heat of the sun, by the lack of food, by an excess of coffee laced with rum, and also by the years of sexual repression. He throws himself into a frenzied, desperate pursuit of Edmée into the deepest part of the forest and forces her to stop. A battle of wills ensues; Bernard is almost overwhelmed by his desire for her but succeeds in running off just in time: 'Edmée n'a jamais su quel péril son honneur a couru dans cette minute d'angoisses' (344). But she is shot anyway, by another Mauprat, Antoine, as though Bernard's desperate desire for total possession has its effect in spite of himself, in what Crecelius calls 'a displaced figuration of Bernard's desire to dominate the proud Edmée' (p. 160).

This part of the novel is full of references to fatality: the fatality of the Mauprat blood, which rises again in Bernard's veins, and the fatality of circumstance, which takes Bernard and Edmée back to the cursed places of their first dramatic meeting, deep in the forest, near both la Roche-Mauprat and the tour Gazeau. In the battle between nature and civilization, fatality and education, the fatality of nature seems to have won. Bernard is back where he started. Everyone believes he is guilty—Patience, Edmée, the abbé Aubert. So even does Marcasse, Bernard's faithful follower, though he never thinks the shooting was intentional. Bernard is banned from Sainte-Sévère where both Edmée and her father lie near death, and forced to remain an outcast at his original home, la Roche-Mauprat. He is ostracised by all who meet him, having become again an untouchable reprobate as his grandfather and uncles were. But he knows he is innocent; he knows and we know that he may have sinned in thought, but that at the last minute the years of his social and moral education came good and helped him survive this supreme test. His stoicism and courage throughout his trial are born of this certainty; and with our assurance of his new, true identity, the novel of education can come to an end. It only remains for the knowledge of his innocence to become public, so that his definitive transformation may be confirmed by all, and particularly by those who guided him through it. So for the last eighty pages, *Mauprat* turns into a detective novel, as Patience, Marcasse and Arthur (who has miraculously appeared) refuse to be satisfied by the unproven assumption of his guilt, the true criminal is hunted out, and Bernard is cleared.

Given the emphasis placed on the different stages of Bernard's development, there is no doubt that *Mauprat* is a novel of education. Yet it also differs in many respects from a more traditional *Bildungsroman* like Stendhal's *Le Rouge et le Noir* or Balzac's *Le Père Goriot*, both written a few years earlier. To begin with, it is only the middle section of the novel which is directly concerned with Bernard's education. As we have seen, he does not really begin to change from the savage that he was until halfway through the narrative (200) and his transformation is in effect complete when he returns to Sainte-Sévère from America eighty pages later. It is true that, provoked by Edmée's continued withdrawal from him, he suffers a brief and terrible relapse into his old ways—'la rechute fut si prompte et si complète' (332)—but he recovers himself through his newly-acquired moral understanding and strength of will, with no help from his former mentors. The novel never suggests that we can change utterly and definitively, and become quite other than what we were. As an old man, Bernard still retains 'une expression de dureté' (37) inherited from his forefathers and is capable of moments of rough impatience with his servants. 'Ne croyez à aucune fatalité absolue et nécessaire, mes enfants', he says at the end, but then adds 'Admettez que nous ne sommes pas toujours absolument libres de choisir entre le bien et le mal' (433). The implication is that his transformation, which he says has taken forty or fifty years and so continued long after the end of his narrative, has gone as far as it could with such a man as he was.

The education proper, then, occupies only eighty pages of text. It is, moreover, mainly concentrated into the first and last years covered by the narrative with only a brief description of the six-year-long, American interlude. This central core is framed by the sinister events which take place at la Roche-Mauprat at the beginning and end of the work, as the novel draws also on the traditions of the *roman noir* and detective fiction. So it appeals in many different ways and on many different levels; Sand appears to introduce her views on education almost incidentally, embodying them within a narrative full of passion and adventure. This contrasts greatly with the systematic, exhaustive account in Rousseau's *Émile*,

for example, and makes it clear that Sand's novel is far from
being a methodical treatise on education.

The differences between this and more traditional
narratives are, however, not only structural. In a
Bildungsroman written by a man, the hero learns how to
succeed in society and eventually to dominate; his love affairs
are simply one of the means he employs to get to the top. He
may at the same time learn much about the nature of love and
the behaviour of women, but this sentimental education is not
usually the prime focus. In *Mauprat*, it is. The values are
reversed; social success (as, for example, in the figure of M. de
la Marche) is despised; the action is largely contained within
the isolated space of Sainte-Sévère among a small group of
privileged people, not on the public stage of the capital city.
From first to last, what Bernard has to learn is appropriate
behaviour with a woman; his intellectual, moral and social
development is directed towards the one end of pleasing
Edmée. He will learn to read and write: for her. He will
comport himself with grace and discretion: for her. He will
fight in the American war of Independence: for her. So the
story of an education becomes a lesson in feminism, and the
male values of action in the world are replaced by a feminine
underscoring of the values of the heart. This *Bildungsroman*,
detective novel, *roman noir*, is also, and perhaps primarily, a
romance.

(iii) Romance

It seems that one of the main differences between the first
and second versions of *Mauprat* is the greater complexity in
the later version of the character of Edmée, who had originally
been already the wife of M. de la Marche and a much more
shadowy figure. It is likely that this was the result of Sand's
involvement at the time in the legal proceedings to ensure her
separation from her husband; these would surely have made
her think more carefully about a woman's situation in
marriage, in particular about how a wife might escape from
her position of inferiority and subservience. In Edmée, she
created a figure who succeeds in inspiring esteem and respect
in her husband as well as lifelong passion, and who therefore

sacrifices nothing when she finally agrees to marry him. Since, however, we see her entirely from Bernard's point of view, any difficulties she may have in combining these different roles of friend and counsellor, and sexual partner, and in reconciling within herself her contradictory feelings can only be guessed at. She is, as Wingård Vareille says (p. 465), trapped within his gaze, and although the gaze of the younger Bernard is in fact often carnal and acquisitive, this view of her is overlaid by a gaze which is consistently ennobling and admiring, which strains all the time to desexualise her, since its owner is always made to feel ashamed of any physical desire he instinctively feels.

This process of idealization begins with Bernard's first view of Edmée when she is brought to la Roche-Mauprat as a sexual conquest by his uncles. Without understanding who she is, he is immediately struck by her difference from the 'insolentes prostituées' or 'victimes stupides' (90) whom he has seen there before. He found and still finds her more beautiful than anybody could ever have imagined: 'Cette femme était belle comme le jour. Je ne crois pas que jamais il ait existé une femme aussi jolie que celle-là' (94). But her beauty is not the typical beauty of her sex; it is combined with 'un air de calme, de franchise et d'honnêteté que je n'avais jamais trouvé sur le front d'aucune autre' (90). He is particularly taken by her hunting-dress, her *amazone*, which he remembers in every detail (136), and which we can see has something masculine about it. Edmée's love of hunting, like that of Indiana, goes against traditional ideas of delicate womanliness since it depends on energy and agility as well as on the excitement of the chase. Indeed, largely unaware of her femininity, she does not play on it, and the young Bernard feels as much the beauty of her character as of her person. She is brave and kind; there is something divine and spiritual about her: 'il semblait que le ciel lui eût donné deux âmes, une toute d'intelligence, une toute de sentiment' (94). Or she is like a fairy out of the chivalric legends told him by his grandfather, remote and ethereal.

He is fascinated but at first too frightened to approach her; then he remembers what his uncles expect of him and, as he says, the wolf rises up in him and he pursues her round the room to take her in his arms. A moment later, he is overcome by respect and adoration and falls to his knees at her feet. Eventually, in her attempts to win him over, she asks him if he

loves her and he says he spoke for the first time as a man, not a
child or a beast, when he cried 'Oui, je t'aime! oui, je t'aime!'
(**105**), implying something more than physical desire. In his
confusion, though, he still wants to possess her and only agrees
to let her go if she will promise to belong to him before
belonging to anybody else. She agrees, but significantly
reverses the order of Bernard's demand by agreeing not to
belong to any one before belonging to him. In this way, she
preserves her right to remain celibate and untouched, although
it will be a long time before Bernard understands the
importance of this reversal. She then insists on his leaving with
her, so that in the end it is she who rescues him as much as he
who saves her. They escape, 'les mains unies en signe de foi
mutuelle' (**109**); in making a pact together, in trusting each
other, they have become equals and allies, not sexual enemies.
Indeed, her behaviour throughout this scene has been the
opposite of that of the typical woman: she has shown neither
weakness nor fear but has mesmerised Bernard through the
power of her personality as much as of her beauty.

Later in the novel, Bernard as narrator interrupts his story
to give a fuller account of Edmée which reinforces his original
view. He describes her as 'une des femmes les plus parfaites
qu'il y eût en France' (**154**). He now emphasises even more her
moral qualities and again seems to see something masculine
about her: 'c'était une fière et intrépide jeune fille autant
qu'une douce et affable châtelaine' (**155**), certainly not a weak
woman to be lusted after and possessed; and she has a good
sense 'au-dessus de son âge, et peut-être de son sexe' (**155**). In
Paris, Bernard contrasts her with the vain, flirtatious and
over-dressed 'femmes du monde' who exaggerate their
womanly charms in order to attract and seduce (**221-4**). Edmée
alone is free of any feminine affectation and eclipses them all,
'dans toute sa fraîcheur de sincérité, dans tout l'éclat de sa
grâce naturelle' (**225**), as she sits on a sofa next to Louis XVI's
minister, Malesherbes. Indeed, later on, Arthur yields to
Bernard's entreaties in naming after her a flower, *Edmea
sylvestris*, that he discovers in the wild American landscape,
thus associating her directly with nature at its purest (**244; 352;
408**).

Her uniqueness lies in her whole person not just in her
physical allure, which is hardly described.There are no scenes
in *Mauprat* equivalent to the bedroom scenes in *Indiana*,

where Raymon's look is openly lascivious as it fastens on the
rich, dark hair and feminine forms of his mistress (whether
Noun or Indiana). The closest we come to this is Bernard's visit
to Edmée's bedroom shortly after his arrival at Sainte-Sévère,
when he feels stifled by the heavy, scented air and disoriented
by the thick carpet and luxurious furniture against which he
stumbles. He seems rather to prefer the displaced veneration of
'Je ne pus passer devant l'appartement d'Edmée sans coller
mes lèvres sur la serrure' (239). He is alarmed by her languor
and pale complexion and hardly dares look at her: he had felt
more at ease with the 'hardiesse virile' (136) she had shown
earlier at la Roche-Mauprat. She is usually described as either
aloof and imperious or as pale and ill, never erotically inviting.
In this way, Sand uses her male narrator to construct an ideal
female figure, whose whole person rejects the very concept of
male desire.

For she is also like a Madonna for whom only a chaste,
Platonic devotion is appropriate. She shows a certain
benevolence towards Bernard, advising him on how to behave
and assuring him of her friendship and esteem, although at
least in their first weeks together she can only allow herself
such intimacy if she is hidden behind the walls of the chapel;
they protect her both literally and figuratively and reinforce
Bernard's view of her as pure and unattainable. He sees her
too as a sister or mother figure whom it would be incestuous to
desire, just as Ralph is both brother and father to Indiana.
When defending her loyalty to him to Aubert, she stresses their
family relationship: 'c'est mon cousin, c'est un Mauprat, c'est
presque un frère' (194). And when he returns from America,
finally civilised, she shows him the tender care of a mother,
insisting on living with him daily on these intimate terms,
apparently unaware of his frustration. Her most important
relationship is with her father towards whom she shows an
exemplary devotion; again it is by a chaste, family tie, between
father and daughter, that she chooses to be defined.

Bozon-Scalzitti makes much of Edmée's maternal role but
sees her as a phallic mother, 'autoritaire, froide, cruelle,
castratrice' (p. 5), that is, a mother who has taken on the role of
the father, lawgiver and emasculator. She is indeed always in
command. Even at their first meeting, when she is effectively
his prisoner, she succeeds in turning the tables on him, by
rewording the promise she makes him and obliging him to

agree. Later that night, at the tour Gazeau, she orders him to keep quiet: 'Rasseyez-vous, tenez-vous tranquille, je vous l'ordonne' (**114**), and this sets the tone for their future dealings. In several key scenes, she subdues and tames him by the brutal coldness of her responses—when he carries her across the river against her will (**147**), or later in Paris when he accuses her of not keeping her word. Most crucially, when he pursues her deep into the forest during the hunt, finally forcing her off her horse and attempting to embrace her, she turns on him, lifting her whip and threatening to lash his face if he so much as touches her. 'C'était une femme intrépide et fière, qui se fût laissé égorger plutot que de permettre une espérance audacieuse' (**341**). In all these scenes, the love story is clearly played out as a battle of wills in which anger almost to the point of hatred is as powerful as love. In the last one, the battle becomes a physical as well as psychological one; by chasing her deeper and deeper into the forest, Bernard is measuring his strength and agility against hers in order to force her to submit. But she is more than his equal and is not afraid to reinforce her moral authority by physical threats, thus meeting him on his own, male ground.

Perhaps the key to Edmée's character is her absolute refusal to submit to any kind of tyranny, in particular the tyranny of a man. Ever since Bernard's arrival at Sainte-Sévère, she has carried a knife, she says (**186**), and plans to take her own life, or his, if she is attacked. She will not trust to her female vulnerability, but defend herself like a man. We hear an echo of Indiana's words to her husband (though not her lover) when Edmée declares to Aubert, in the conversation overheard by Bernard: 'je ne souffrirai jamais la tyrannie de l'homme, pas plus la violence d'un amant que le soufflet d'un mari', recalling the fate of her namesake—'Sainte Solange, *la belle pastoure,* se laissa trancher la tête plutôt que de subir le droit du seigneur'—but suggesting she will put up more determined resistance than the other two victims (**189-90**). Sand had herself been slapped by her husband and never forgave him for her public humiliation; and this proud independence is what makes of her heroines exemplary feminist figures, particularly Edmée, whose moments of weakness are rare. Indeed, by the end, her victory over Bernard is complete; for, although equality is clearly all-important in this book, their marriage is not in fact a marriage of equals. Bernard, as narrator, makes it clear that she was always the stronger, that he followed her advice in everything: 'Pour moi, je puis dire que mon éducation fut faite par elle; pendant tout le cours de ma vie je m'abandonnai entièrement à sa raison et à sa droiture' (431). The emphasis is always on his devotion to her, which never wavers: 'dans le passé, dans le présent, dans l'avenir'. We can only assume that it was returned but are never quite sure. Indeed there are many details we are not given in these last, extremely brief pages of the book which describe their married life. Although their relationship must have been a sexual one since they have six children (unlike Ralph and Indiana), Bernard says not a word of any physical happiness between them. This is entirely suppressed, perhaps because it would have implied submission on Edmée's part, or because of Sand's own anxiety about sex. All that is described of their thirty years of marriage (in eight pages) is her complete control over his public activities, so that we are left with the image of a strong, independent wife, who is totally in command: the reverse of the contemporary, conventional view of her role. Herein lies the most important message of the book, a feminist rather than a socialist one since it implies female dominance rather than a simple equality with men.

But perhaps there is another way to read this novel, an alternative story which is much less clear-cut, the story of Edmée's internal conflict, of which Bernard has no inkling. Although he finds much of her behaviour puzzling, he is so caught beneath her spell that he usually dares not question it further. She frequently looks at him, as he says, 'd'un air étrange', 'avec une expression singulière' or with 'un regard mystérieux'; apparently her comportment at Sainte-Sévère has changed to such an extent since Bernard's arrival that even the abbé Aubert has noticed: 'il y a quelque chose d'étrange [...] et de forcé en elle, qui n'est pas du tout dans sa manière d'être accoutumée' (149). When Bernard tries to read her thoughts, he comes up against a blank wall: 'Sa physionomie n'exprimait alors qu'une patiente curiosité et la volonté inébranlable de lire jusqu'au fond de mon âme sans me laisser voir seulement la surface de la sienne' (331). Elsewhere she tells Aubert that she does not even understand herself and cannot say why she acts as she does. Her behaviour is most baffling on Bernard's return from America, modest, sensitive and responsible, as she had always wished *him* to be. Yet still she refuses to commit herself,

thus provoking in him a frustration which almost ends in
terrible disaster. Can we as readers decipher her better than
Bernard, her father, or the abbé Aubert? Can we understand
why she refuses to leave Bernard behind at la Roche-Mauprat,
but seven years later will still not be his wife? Why does she
keep deferring marriage, having dismissed her former fiancé?
Why is she so often sad and ill? Is it possible for us to
reconstruct her story in a way that makes sense, or must we
also accept that she is fickle and irrational, as women are
supposed to be?

She herself tells Aubert that her behaviour may be explained
by her fear of Bernard's violence combined with her strong
sense of honour, which will not allow her to desert him; hence
her frequent shifts from kindness to coldness and back. Bernard
interprets as fear her reaction to his sudden, violent sweeping
of her into his arms in order to carry her across the river, but it
is probable that her withdrawal from him is not caused simply
by fear of his physical roughness but by an aversion to being
dominated in any way by him (or by any man). This is the
reason Wingård Vareille suggests for her refusal to marry him
on his return from America: now that he has become an adult,
she realises she has no excuses left but is still reluctant to
compromise her freedom and independence (p. 430). Earlier,
she had given her duty to her father as another reason not to
proceed. Perhaps all the tests she sets him are not only part of
an educational programme but also a means of deferring her
marriage for as long as possible. Perhaps her periods of
unexplained sadness are caused not by disappointment in him
but by her realisation that she will soon run out of grounds for
delay.

Fear is often accompanied by anger; and there is no doubt
that Edmée is exasperated by Bernard's over-familiarity in
carrying her across the river. She resists any assumption of
intimacy, just as she resists any reference he makes to her vow
to him at la Roche-Mauprat during the angry scene in Paris,
for example. She will not be forced into anything. Indeed,
Dayan sees nothing but contempt and revulsion in her attitude
to Bernard during their first meeting (1, p. 59); and her
irritation at his violence is clear enough when he forces her off
her horse at the climax of the hunt scene, the more so as,
clumsily, his lips 'effleurèrent son sein' (340).

Or perhaps she is playing with him out of perversity and in order to make him jealous. Bernard himself offers this explanation one evening in Paris when she teases him, as she picks the petals off an aster, to guess who it is who loves her 'un peu, beaucoup, passionnément' or 'pas du tout' (**230**). She certainly does seem to be goading him here, cruelly and unnecessarily, since she knows very well of his love for her and jealousy of M. de la Marche. But why should she do this? After all, at their first meeting, Bernard had described her as the opposite of coquettish, as possessed of 'un air de calme, de franchise et d'honnêteté' (**90**). What has changed her so much? At his trial, she herself gives the same explanation for her behaviour throughout: 'Beaucoup de femmes pensent que ce n'est pas un grand crime d'avoir un peu de coquetterie avec l'homme qu'on aime' (**412**); and again 'elle s'accusa généreusement de tous mes torts, et prétendit que, si nous avions eu des querelles, c'était parce qu'elle y prenait un secret plaisir, parce qu'elle y voyait la force de mon amour' (**413**). She even explains her anger with him during the hunt just before the shooting as 'une *petite colère de femme assez niaise*' (**409**). But can we believe her? She is evidently intent on clearing Bernard's name publicly by declaring that she had always loved him. Arthur had interpreted her odd behaviour quite differently; for him, she was setting Bernard a series of tests which were anything but capricious and illogical, but intended to allow him to prove himself, expiate his faults and thus merit her love. But it is clear that he does not fully understand her either; his view takes no account of her weaknesses and contradictions.

The only way to reconcile all these interpretations is to ascribe her actions to her passion for Bernard and to see this passion as riven by conflict between 'l'esprit romanesque' and 'l'humeur très fière' (**414**), and so likely to produce intense, emotional responses and erratic behaviour. There are hints of her (possibly sexual) attraction to him right from the beginning; she promises never to desert him and kisses him on the cheek 'avec effusion' (although this may also be out of gratitude for his help). Her later reiteration to him and to Aubert of her strong sense of loyalty to him—'je ne souffrirai pas qu'on le chasse de cette maison; j'en sortirai plutôt moi-même' (**194**)— seems unnecessarily emphatic, as though inspired by something more than pity and pride, perhaps by a powerful need for his physical presence. When she tells her maid, mademoiselle Leblanc, that she preferred him as he had been at la Roche-Mauprat, dirty and unkempt, to the well-dressed creature he had been transformed into (138), we sense that she is attracted to his virility as well as frightened of it. It is this sexual feeling she is fighting, because she sees it as a weakness threatening her independence and control. Much later she ascribes it to an irresistible fatality. Michèle Hecquet compares her love to a kind of castration which drains her of her vital energy, represented symbolically in the two episodes when she is wounded and her blood flows (p. 61). So what we see are the outward signs of her desperate internal conflict, a conflict which weakens and exhausts her all the more because it cannot be spoken of: hence her moments of sadness and languor, when she retreats entirely into herself.

She changes most dramatically during the six years of Bernard's exile in America: 'elle avait fait plus que de dompter son caractère, elle avait changé jusqu'à la circulation de son sang' (277). Again we are not told precisely why. Is it because she has been consumed by her frustrated passion for Bernard? Or is it, more mundanely as the narrator suggests, that she has been forced to spend all her time with her increasingly ailing father, and so has lacked air and exercise? But perhaps that devotion to her father which used fully to satisfy her emotional needs is no longer enough. Crecelius sees the development of both Edmée and Bernard as examples of the working out of the Oedipus complex, as each transfers his or her love from parent figure to sexual partner, Edmée here acting as both mother and lover to Bernard (p. 157). This is perhaps clearest in Edmée's case, as her love for Bernard increases in proportion to the gradual waning of her father's strength and influence. Her near-fatal illness after the shooting is paralleled by that of her father, but whereas he dies of it, she is reborn into a new life. Like Bernard's earlier, her illness can be seen as a rite of passage which purges her of her conflicting emotions so that she can move on, strengthened and elevated, from the confusions of the past to the certainties of the future. Only after this can she definitively and publicly affirm her undying passion. The opposing aspects of her personality, her weakness and her strength, her body and her mind, do not remain in contradiction as in *Indiana* but are eventually resolved into an ideal harmony, although this is never described. As we have

seen, 'de telles années ne se racontent pas' (**430**); there is
nothing to say about Utopia except that it is perfect.

The reader is fully convinced that Edmée has always loved
Bernard only a few pages from the end of the book, when the
abbé Aubert repeats the remainder of his earlier conversation
with her. Of course this adds to the suspense, but it also
relegates to the margins the issue of a woman's passion and
the conflicts it can engender. We may presume that Sand
structured her novel in this way, using Bernard as her sole
narrator, so that the anxiety that can be suffered by a woman
in love with a virile man does not overshadow the optimism of
the final message. We are less troubled by Bernard's distress,
since it clearly stems from egoism and insensitivity which he
will learn to correct; Edmée's distress is intrinsic to her
situation. In many ways, the novel is a moral tale which ends
with an ideal view of marriage, but Sand wished also to
include some of the difficulties encountered on the way, in
particular the difficulties of a woman, as she herself was
experiencing them in her relationship with Michel de Bourges
(by whom she felt dominated and betrayed). As Edmée fights
against a love she finds demeaning, so Sand too was torn by
her contradictory feelings for her lover, although for her they
were never finally resolved.

(iv) Socialism

The third important strand in *Mauprat's* complex thematic
structure is Sand's socialist vision, which extends the
significance of her personal concerns—with marriage and
education—by embedding them in a wider, historical context.
The main action of the novel takes place in the 1770s and 1780s,
and the epilogue carries us through to the 1830s, dealing very
briefly with the period of the French Revolution and its
aftermath. The same ideals of progress and enlightenment
which are highlighted through the story of the protagonists are
also important in the historical background, so that the one
parallels and reinforces the other. Bernard's development is
symbolic of the development of the century towards greater
equality and respect for others, since he represents Everyman
as well as his individual self. Although the main events occur

before the Revolution, there are many prophetic allusions to what is to come, and the confrontations at Bernard's trial can be seen as symbolic of the Revolution itself. By suppressing any direct account of the years 1789 to 1794, however, Sand avoids dealing directly with the violence and bloodshed of the Terror, and is able to keep her idealism intact. The story of Bernard and Edmée ends in a Utopian paradise apart from the world, but the reality of history inevitably casts doubts on the optimism of this conclusion.

It is particularly through the character of the peasant Patience that Sand develops her idealised vision of the future. He is compared to Socrates, and symbolises in his development and his final role what the people can accomplish. It seems that he was the central figure in the first version of the novel, which is thought to have consisted of the present chapters III, IV and V, describing his character, philosophy and the incident with the owl. So the socialist vision was at the origin of the text; the concerns with education and marriage came later, and eventually took over as Sand's proccupations changed. By considering these too as expanded illustrations of the original social theme, as examples of man's perfectibility in the private and public sphere, we can better grasp their general as well as their simply personal significance.

When we first meet Patience, he is living in voluntary exile in the tour Gazeau, a ruined tower deep in the forest near the castle of la Roche-Mauprat. Although a poor peasant, he is also an eccentric Rousseau-like figure, a 'philosophe rustique' (59) who has rejected the conventional education of the church and retired from the world. Hardly able to read and refusing all book learning, he is nonetheless wise and contemplative, professing a natural philosophy which stresses the importance of living according to nature and includes a belief in the innate principles of justice and equality. His only mentor is the Jansenist Aubert, also rejected by the Church for his unorthodox views, who introduces him to the religious and social ideas of Rousseau's *Profession de foi d'un vicaire savoyard* and *Du contrat social*, with which he already seems remarkably in tune. Again we see the importance of Rousseau as the guiding spirit behind the text as a whole. This spiritual and philosophical awareness is later complemented by an intuitive love of poetry, in particular that of Tasso, Homer and

Dante, first read to him by Edmée and which he now knows by heart.

A totally idealised and unreal figure, unlike any character in *Indiana*, he unashamedly embodies all Sand's own beliefs: the value of imagination, intuition and sensation rather than reason, the presence of the divine in nature, and man's perfectibility. He is a fluent orator, and his language is a strange amalgam of the vigorous and authentic idioms of the peasant with the most richly expressive images of poetry. This is very like the style which Sand seeks in her rural novels, a blend of literary sophistication and genuine, popular *berrichon* expressions. He is also a prophet of the future; the local peasants see him as a wizard, a 'sorcier' (**70**), endow him with magic powers, and both respect and fear him. They call him 'Patience' because of his frequent mutterings of the word as he tries to contain his impatience at the social inequalities he sees around him (**74**). The name is important since it suggests the necessarily slow pace of change as envisaged by Patience (and Sand); revolutions should be gradual and progressive, allowed to happen naturally and therefore peacefully. Again, the sudden and extreme eruptions of violence during the revolutionary years are set aside by this emphasis on restraint.

Patience's conduct during the incident of the owl seems to anticipate the Revolution to come some twelve years later and his own attitude to it. The young aristocrat, Bernard, is punished for his cruel arrogance in gratuitously stoning Patience's pet owl by being tied to a tree so that the blood of the owl drips down upon his head. In the same way, during the Terror, the aristocracy will be made to pay in blood for its former cruelties. But unlike the *sans-culottes*, Patience quickly takes pity on his victim and unties him; he is more exemplary than representative, and demonstrates Sand's own compassion and dislike of violence. Later in the book, having recognised the potential for good in Bernard, he reveals to him the realities of social inequality and delivers an eloquent prophecy of the inevitable changes to come:

> Le pauvre a assez souffert; il se tournera contre le riche, et les châteaux tomberont, et les terres seront dépecées. Je ne verrai pas cela, mais vous le verrez; il y aura dix chaumières à la place de ce parc, et dix familles vivront de son revenu. Il n'y aura plus ni valets, ni maîtres, ni vilains, ni seigneurs. (**178**)

He does not remain the wild man of the woods. Encouraged by Edmée, he moves into a small cottage with its own garden on the edge of the park of Sainte-Sévère, halfway between nature and civilization, and acts as her intermediary in her gifts of charity to the local peasants. His development in some ways parallels that of Bernard, who also moved from the savage solitude of la Roche-Mauprat to the cultivated environment of Sainte-Sévère, to be raised up and educated by Edmée. He is both an educator (of Bernard) and educated himself (by Edmée). These three characters are linked by all kinds of similarities and contrasts of temperament and situation; most importantly for the message of the book, the bond between Edmée and Patience suggests a possible future alliance between the aristocracy and the people. This was a favourite dream of Sand, who represented that alliance in her own person, being born of an aristocratic father and a plebeian mother. In fact, of course, particularly after the July Revolution of 1830, power came to rest with neither class but with the bourgeoisie, whom Sand hated for their materialism and complacency. Hence the novel demonstrates how things might have been, not how they were, a typical feature of her creative disagreements with Balzac, who did the opposite.

By far the oddest figure in the novel is that of Marcasse, who seems intended as a popular type but whose eccentricities make him much more of a comic caricature than a social symbol. As Patience's friend and ally, we would expect him to complement him as another representative of the people; and indeed in some ways he does. His muteness sets off Patience's eloquence; his physical agility as rat, mole and weasel-catcher contrasts with his friend's contemplative, visionary nature. He is constantly in society rather than withdrawn from it, literally cleansing the great aristocratic houses of their vermin although unable to change their natures. As much of a visionary as his friend, he demonstrates his idealism by doing rather than being and thinking. He is inspired to fight on the side of the Americans in their war of independence and becomes Bernard's sergeant, serving him with total fidelity during the war, and after in his battles with his surviving brothers and with society. His final legendary feat is to cross a yawning chasm between the ruined castle of la Roche-Mauprat and a tower in which the fugitive Antoine Mauprat is hiding by inching along a fire-damaged beam that is barely able

to take a man's weight: 'Le jour se levait et dessinait dans l'air
grisâtre la silhouette effilée et la démarche modeste et fière de
l'hidalgo' (419). His capture of Antoine finally and definitively
clears Bernard's name.

Yet our first, much earlier view of Marcasse in the tour
Gazeau reminds us irrepressibly of the figure of Don Quixote
as portrayed by Daumier, for example:

> ... un chapeau à grands bords ombrageait un cône olivâtre
> terminé par une maigre barbe, et le mur recevait la silhouette
> d'un nez tellement effilé qu'il n'y avait rien au monde qui
> pût lui être comparé, si ce n'est une longue rapière posée en
> travers sur les genoux du personnage, et la face d'un petit
> chien qu'on eût prise à sa forme pointue pour celle d'un rat
> gigantesque: si bien qu'il regnait une harmonie mystérieuse
> entre ces trois pointes acérées, le nez de Don Marcasse, le
> museau de son chien et la lame de son épée. (111)

The various lines and angles drawn by his nose, the rapier, and
the pointed muzzle of his little dog give a strikingly visual
picture, and this is reinforced by other later descriptions, the
rotten beam in his final exploit providing yet another
horizontal to complete the design. Indeed, in his physical
person as well as his idealism, he is later compared explicitly to
Don Quixote by Bernard. But Don Quixote was a mad
aristocrat, anything but a representative of the people, and he
failed at every enterprise he undertook. What is he doing in a
novel about personal enlightenment and social progress?
Perhaps he is there to remind us that *Mauprat* is a fable about
extraordinary people attempting to create their own Utopia,
not a realistic social programme; we may see him as part of
Sand's Utopia, which is able to accommodate the comic and
fantastic as well as the ideal.

The American War of Independence of the 1770s serves as
another vehicle for Sand's socialist views, while avoiding any
reference to the violence that accompanied their realisation in
France, particularly since the focus is not on the war itself but
on the ideals of the pacific botanist, Arthur. She sees the revolt
against colonialism as exemplary of a new spirit of democracy
which was sweeping across Europe and America, and as a
prefiguration of the French Revolution itself. But when the
Revolution does actually erupt, it seems to happen far away
from the idyllic intimacy enjoyed by the protagonists: 'Les

orages de la révolution ne détruisirent point notre existence, et les passions qu'elle souleva ne troublèrent pas l'union de notre intérieur' (431). They survey it from afar, recognizing the greatness of the vision behind it while regretting the cruelty and bloodshed that went with it. Bernard and Edmée play their part by gladly giving up a large part of their property to the new republic, but otherwise remain strangely untouched. Patience is the only one to play an active role: elected as judge in his district, he manages to perform his functions without sacrificing any of the idealism which marked him out before. He remains as principled, as impartial, as wise and firm as ever. All possible problems are ignored; the real world of difficult decisions and morally ambiguous actions is far from the Utopianism of this conclusion.

Crecelius sees Bernard's trial as 'emblematic' of the Revolution of 1789 itself, the account of it an alternative to a direct description of the violent confrontations to come (p. 153). It is indeed a fitting climax to the novel, the point at which the different strands come together and the various stories are resolved. Bernard's transformation is proven by his brave and dignified acceptance of society's unjust treatment and the threat of the death penalty. He sees fatality at work in the forces ranged against him and accepts at this point that in the end fate may be stronger than the individual, although he knows very well that fate can take on a human, and most prejudicial, form: 'Dans tout le cours de l'affaire, une main invisible dirigea tout avec une célérité et une âpreté implacables' (362). All that matters to him is that Edmée should believe in his innocence and see him as finally worthy of her love. So the romance too is satisfactorily concluded by Edmée's public avowal of her passion for him. For after her illness, which is the ultimate test of her resolve to deny him, she ceases to fight against her love and admits its overwhelming power. She realises the need to declare these most private feelings in public, going against both the conventions of feminine modesty and her own instinctive reserve, since what is essentially being debated 'dans ce froid aréopage' is the question 'Est-il aimé, ou n'est-il pas aimé?' (415). The intense emotions during the drama of her court appearances confirm how far she has had to step out of her womanly role in responding to so public an interrogation. It now only remains for their marriage to be solemnised as conclusive proof that each is worthy of the other;

and the natural and sexual bond between them becomes also a legal one.

Most importantly, the trial acts out the bitter battles between opposing sections of society, in which good is allowed to triumph. On the one side stands the Catholic Church, represented by the prior of the Trappist monastery and by brother Népomucène, Jean Mauprat in disguise. Hypocritical and greedy for money, they insidiously wield great power with the local people and have bought off various important witnesses. Theirs is the 'main invisible' which Bernard sees as manipulating events behind the scenes. The legal system acts in collusion with the Church, expediting the proceedings with undue haste so that Bernard's defence has no time to collect evidence in his favour. These are the two vested interests which are seen as crucially supporting the *ancien régime*. Sand is much more bitterly critical of them than of the aristocracy itself, which in her idealistic view is potentially enlightened and capable of altruism. On the other side stands Patience, the peasant, who insists on a delay so that further evidence can be gathered, and demands a second trial in the name of the people's love of truth and justice: 'Mettez-vous à genoux, hommes du peuple, mes frères, mes enfants; priez, suppliez, obtenez que justice soit faite et colère réprimée. C'est votre devoir, c'est votre droit et votre intérêt; c'est vous qu'on insulte et qu'on menace quand on viole les lois' (387). At this point, he stands alone, though with the silent support of the abbé Aubert, who has been put in prison for his refusal to testify against Bernard.

For the second trial he is joined by Arthur, recently arrived from America and representative of the new spirit cf liberalism from across the ocean, and Edmée, whom Arthur has successfully persuaded to appear in court. Thus Bernard is defended by those sections of society which were powerless at the time but which Sand saw as the great forces of the future— the democrat, the people and women. Of these, the most practically important is the voice of the people, represented by Patience; it is his commitment to finding out the true criminal that finally exonerates Bernard from any crime, although it is important that his testimony is given before that of Edmée, whose passion for Bernard finally convinces the court of his worth. For it is her love that proves definitively not just that he did not commit this particular crime, but that he is a fundamentally changed person and her moral equal. Love finally triumphs against the forces of evil, not just love between men and women but between all individuals and all classes. The heterogeneous group of friends now refuse to be separated—Bernard and Edmée, with Patience, Arthur, the abbé Aubert and Marcasse, through whose intrepid, practical action the true criminal is actually seized. 'Nous montâmes tous dans la même voiture de voyage [...;] nous les traitâmes sur le pied de la plus parfaite égalité. Jamais dès lors, ils n'eurent d'autre table que la nôtre' (423-4) They have indeed created their own Utopia, though when their story is told Bernard alone is still alive to bear witness to it.

(v) Narrative frame

It is impossible to make full sense of a novel without taking into account the perspective from which the story is being told. Is the narrator speaking directly on behalf of the author or do we need to allow for his own personal bias? Is his personality part of the substance of the text or does it stand outside it? The conventions of realism assume that the narrator is a kind of historian, authoritative and all-knowing, though even in the canonical texts of Balzac and Stendhal things are not always so simple. We have already seen the difficulties Sand had in *Indiana* in reconciling this narrative convention with her own personal (female) angle. By openly employing a first-person perspective in *Mauprat* she avoids the possibility of any confusion between the subjective and objective, the internal and external, yet the text does not thereby become completely transparent and unified. It is true that the story is told almost entirely in Bernard's voice, but that voice is itself split, and may also be being used for several different purposes by the author. His double and changing view of Edmée has already been discussed, and it is also clear that a different weight should be accorded to the accounts of Patience's history and character he gives at different times. We still need to be on our guard, aware of the sleight of hand used by authors of fictional texts.

As in *Indiana*, Sand has chosen a male narrator, although here he is quite clearly a character within the story. Why did she not adopt a female perspective since this novel obviously falls outside the conventions of nineteenth-century realism? Why did she not recount the action from Edmée's point of view, using her own personal experience more directly? The novel might have been all the more powerful and credible as a result, although she would have been also going against the convention of the earlier *roman personnel*, which, as we have seen, almost always used a male voice. Perhaps she wished to put her feminist message across more clearly and simply, to convince male readers of woman's potential by exploiting their sympathy with Bernard's admiring devotion rather than reminding them of her weaknesses (as does the narrator of *Indiana*). On the other hand, by patently using a voice other than her own, by declaring to Gustave Papet that it is 'un conte qui n'est pas nouveau pour toi' (**34**), that is to say, to quote Martine Reid (p. 44), a '«mensonge»', she seems to be denying any responsibility for the feminist and socialist convictions which Bernard finally espouses. Are we supposed to agree or disagree with Bernard at the end when he differs from Rousseau (and Edmée) on the question of man's original goodness? Whom and what are we to believe? Whatever the answer (and we are certainly inclined to believe Bernard), there is no doubt that, since all points of view are necessarily subjective, the novel gains in authenticity and subtlety by abandoning the certainties of an unambiguously didactic text.

It takes a while for the main first-person narration to get going. We start with the 1851 'Notice', followed by the dedication to Gustave Papet, both of which are in Sand's voice and establish the work's status as fiction set deep in the Berry countryside, 'dans les chaumières de notre Vallée Noire' (**34**). When the novel proper begins, we still remain at a distance from the central narrator, for the second voice is that of the '*petit* jeune homme' (**39**), as Bernard calls him, whose roots are also in the Berry and who has heard there 'des histoires à faire dresser les cheveux sur la tête' (**36**). Not that this story is one of these; it is 'une narration [...] noire' (**37**), but there is something consoling about it. It is not fiction but fact, the life story of Bernard Mauprat, although its setting in the context of stories of Bluebeard and other bogeymen lends it some of the aura of fable. Perhaps the '*petit* jeune homme', is again Sand but in disguise; like him, she was small in stature, known to wear men's clothes, and loved to listen to the tales told by the local peasants. Or perhaps she is his friend, the second narratee, who introduces him to Bernard, now finally allowed to embark on his own 'histoire de ma vie' with these two young men as audience. This gradual lead-in, with its odd mixture of the fabulous and the real, draws us into the world of the novel and encourages us to suspend our disbelief. Stirred by this tale from the local countryside, we identify with the two narratees. We can see Bernard as an old man, welcoming and intimidating at the same time and feel the immediacy and power of his oral narration. The illusion is maintained throughout as the narrative occasionally pauses for Bernard to recover from his emotion, or for the two young men to refresh themselves with a cup of the coffee their host no longer drinks, although they are not allowed to speak (as they do in some other first-person narratives of this kind). It is only Bernard's voice that we hear, unremitting, nostalgic and disturbing.

Another important effect of this narrative frame is to open up temporal vistas that go beyond the eight years directly covered by the action. The novel begins in the present of the first narrator, when the castle of la Roche-Mauprat is already in ruins, destroyed by its present owner in an attempt to wipe out its terrible inheritance. This inheritance, however, is then resurrected through the narrative of that owner, Bernard, a figure from the past, whose person and life story form a bridge between past and present. We are now in the 1830s, but he speaks in the reflective, sometimes sentimental, sometimes ironic tone of the eighteenth century about a woman who represented all the values of the Enlightenment. He understands that the young narrator is 'observateur et narrateur', indeed a professional, and, like Ralph at the end of *Indiana*, asks him to tell his story to the world so that he may be fully exonerated: 'Un homme aussi infortuné que je l'ai été mérite de trouver un historiographe fidèle, qui lave sa mémoire de tout reproche' (39). So the novel reaches into the future, handing down the ethos of leisured civilization and moralizing spirit of the eighteenth century into the more positivist and pragmatic nineteenth century, just as Edmée's and Bernard's children will carry the name of Mauprat into the future.

Yet, particularly in the universalizing reflections of the epilogue, Bernard seems to speak from a perspective outside time; it is thirty years since he has been in the world and no mention is made of the historical changes during that period, of Napoleon's reign and defeat, the Restoration and the July monarchy. He is also speaking from a neutral space, from neither la Roche-Mauprat, now in ruins, nor Sainte-Sévère, which was presumably lost to them during the Revolution. Instead we learn that 'il habite une jolie maison de campagne vers Châteauroux, en pays de plaine' (37), a sunny, open place with no dark secrets or painful memories. We are never told when and why he moved there; we know that his marriage took place at Sainte-Sévère and we assume that this is where the couple lived at first, so the chronological gap is paralleled by a spatial gap, both of which have the effect of enclosing the text within itself, giving it a dreamlike quality, removed from our present place and time. It is not a story about our reality, or even the reality of Sand's contemporaries, but a fable or an allegory whose moral message is universal, more like *La Nouvelle Héloïse* (with Edmée as Julie and Bernard as Saint-Preux) than *Le Rouge et le Noir*.

From the outset, Bernard's status is exemplary. His very telling of his story in a tone that is meditative and composed proves that it has ended well, that he is no longer the beast of la Roche-Mauprat but a fully rational man of the Enlightenment. The conclusion is already contained in the beginning, so that we read of his education and his passion for Edmée knowing of their happy end; the optimism of the final message implicitly informs the whole text. Occasionally Bernard exploits his retrospective knowledge of the future to widen the significance of the present moment. For example, he gives us a premonition of the difficulties (similar to those encountered by Indiana—*supra*, p. 24) he will face as he enters society: 'Je ne savais pas les usages du monde où j'entrais' (181); or he foresees his eventual painful abandonment of his aristocratic sense of rank: 'J'ai partagé longtemps cette conviction; elle était dans mon sang, si je puis m'exprimer ainsi. Je ne l'ai perdue qu'à la suite des rudes leçons de ma destinée' (129). There is a flashforward to the time when plebeian qualities such as Patience's will come to the fore: 'La révolution française a fait savoir depuis ce temps qu'il y avait dans le peuple de fougueuses éloquences et une implacable logique' (179). He heightens the atmosphere of foreboding towards the end by hinting at the catastrophic re-emergence of the two surviving Mauprat brothers. 'Vous n'en avez peut-être pas fini avec les Mauprat', says Aubert, and the narrator adds ominously and succinctly at the end of a chapter: 'Le pauvre

abbé ne croyait pas dire si vrai' (312). Bernard, as narrator, brings the future into the present to give a sense of linearity and coherence and to show that things sometimes turn out differently from what we expect. We know that his is a success story but are made aware of the uncertainty and pain that also await him.

What are Bernard's motives for embarking on his narrative in the first place, he who 'ne parle pas facilement de moi' (39)? Do we need to take these into account in our assessment of what he says? There is no doubt that his main reason, perhaps in imitation of Rousseau's *Confessions*, is to explain and defend himself, in order to be remembered as the person he became rather than the beast he was. Yet this may prove to be more difficult than he anticipates, since he is still not sure he understands the significance of his scapegrace life. This is yet another reason for him to re-examine his experience, and in the Conclusion I shall seek to establish his success in drawing a clear lesson. These motivations may be seen to complement each other, since the first suggests a subjective account and the second demands total objectivity. Also implicit throughout the narrative is Bernard's desperate need to celebrate the woman he loved and still loves uniquely, to preserve for ever his image of her and share it with the world. These different motivations account for the shifts of tone and perspective in the single narrative voice, all of which need to be studied if the novel is to be properly understood.

In fact, Bernard's attitude to his younger self is somewhat ambiguous. He is aware of how the few finer feelings he has become deadened by the casual brutality of his kinsmen:

> Sous ma grossière enveloppe, mon cœur n'avait sans doute que des tressaillements de peur et de dégoût à l'aspect des supplices [...]. Cependant, avec le temps, je me blasai un peu sur ces impressions terribles. (57)

He is particularly ashamed of his early arrogance with Patience and his overweening vanity in society when he had acquired a smattering of education. He recognises the injustice of his resentment of the well-meaning, if wrong-headed, abbé Aubert. On the other hand, he insists that he was not all bad and refuses even now to express remorse for his early crimes: 'Je ne vous ferai point d'excuses; mais vous voyez devant vous un homme qui a fait le métier de bandit. C'est un souvenir qui ne me laisse nul remords, pas plus qu'à un soldat d'avoir fait campagne sous les ordres de son général' (85). He even seems proud of his bravado when he met Patience for the second time, and shocks us later by his easy disparagement of the peasant's intelligence and will. 'Patience se débattit jusqu'à la mort dans les ténèbres d'une ignorance dont il ne voulait ni ne pouvait sortir' (160). This hardly squares with the admiration for Patience expressed elsewhere. Sometimes these different perspectives can be explained as belonging to the younger or older Bernard, each of whom has a different voice, although in the last example, at least, the narrator seems to have retained some of his earlier contempt for the visionary peasant, just as he insists on maintaining throughout his first, over-simplified, idealizing view of Edmée.

There are occasions too when Bernard steps out of his role as active participant in the drama and adopts the stance of the omniscient narrator. Although he could well have later acquired the information he gives on Patience's early life or on the reasons for Marcasse's departure for America, the necessarily detached and reflective tone he adopts at these moments is rather different from the personal voice of the rest of the narrative. Sand clearly recognised the discrepancy, since at one point she draws attention to the contrasting perspectives of past and present: 'Après ce récit de la vie philosophique de Patience, rédigé par l'homme d'aujourd'hui, [...] j'ai quelque peine à retourner aux impressions bien différentes que reçut l'homme d'autrefois en rencontrant le sorcier de la tour Gazeau' (68). It seems too that Patience adopts an omniscient voice, Sand's, when he explains at length to Bernard the temperament and conduct of the local tenants; he is going beyond his function even of visionary peasant here, and speaks almost as a sociologist and economist.

There are several scenes involving Bernard's overhearing of private conversations, which he repeats verbatim to his audience of narratees; in this way Sand is able to escape the limits of a single viewpoint, just as she does in using an omniscient voice to give us Patience's life story. Sometimes she integrates the device into the action by suggesting that Bernard was changed by what he overheard, as in the case of the conversation between Edmée and Aubert, but just as often, Bernard's presence behind the bushes can be seen as a fictional device. He seems to spend his time spying on other people—

'j'allais rôder cependant dans les taillis'; 'caché dans les touffes d'un if monstrueux' (161)—or he happens to be in the right place at the right time, half asleep in the grass, when he hears Edmée pronounce his name. And yet such scenes are also consistent with Bernard's character at that time: his closeness to nature and his wariness of others.

Sand exploits the first-person narrative with some skill, allowing it to cover harmoniously a range of perspectives. The psychological richness of the adult Bernard gives a crucial extra dimension to the portrayal of his younger self by demonstrating how far he has changed and how far he has remained the same. It also lends an immediacy and coherence to the text, at the same time setting it up as a moral allegory, since Bernard punctuates his account with philosophical considerations on man's innate nature and the importance of education. He says he is an ordinary man, 'ni métaphysicien, ni psychologue, ni philosophe' (53), but in fact his attitude is that of an eighteenth-century *philosophe:* hence one man's experience becomes a lesson for us all.

Conclusion

One of the main differences between *Mauprat* and *Indiana* is the greater importance in *Mauprat* of the moral message. In *Indiana* it is only one factor among many and is often at odds with more specifically literary aspects of the text: the narrative voice, for example, or the character of Indiana. In *Mauprat*, characterization, structure and point of view, together with elements from the various genres which the novel exploits, all contribute to the overall meaning, enriching and qualifying without undermining it. We may still feel, however, that there are questions left unanswered, uncertainties unresolved as to the nature of the moral example and its application.

The lesson most evidently implied by the conclusion of the novel is that of man's perfectibility, of the ever-present possibility of improvement, not through violent change but through education and love. We shall always be determined to some extent by our basic natures and early experiences (Bernard never completely rids himself of his hotheadedness), but these can be tempered and redirected over a lifetime

towards a higher level of altruism and civilisation. 'Ne croyez
à aucune fatalité absolue et nécessaire' (433), Bernard tells his
young audience in one of the most significant statements of the
book. We all have certain essential tendencies, but these can be
largely dominated and overridden to make the world a better
place. The most important influence for good during this
process is that of a woman, who is regarded by Bernard (and
apparently Sand) as the source of all morality. Edmée has an
instinctive idealism and compassion for others which make her
the best leader of men, so that although she believes
unquestioningly in the importance of equality, there is no doubt
that at the end she dominates all around her. This ideal society
is matriarchal rather than patriarchal (her father has died), but
perhaps not yet fully fraternal.

The final message contradicts Sand's socialism in another
way too, since the small community with which the novel
concludes clearly consists of exceptional people. Again, Edmée
seems to see no contradiction with her views on equality: 'Nous
étions deux caractères d'exception, il nous fallait des amours
héroïques; les choses ordinaires nous eussent rendus méchants
l'un et l'autre' (428). It is difficult to view Patience and
Marcasse either as ordinary representatives of the people or as
in any way realistic; their qualities and attributes elevate them
high above their class and ensure they are worthy of the
respect accorded them by the heroic protagonists. Only the
abbé Aubert falls a little short, but even he shows a loyalty and
integrity above the average when put to the test. These five
characters are clearly marked out from the rest, the stupid and
corrupt mademoiselle Leblanc (no sorority here!) or the weak
and greedy peasants whom Edmée and Patience try to help,
and one wonders whether the moral idealism of the little group
of friends in any way implies a belief in a wider form of
democracy. It is true that we have moved one step on from the
Utopian couple with which Indiana concludes; at least this
community still lives in France and extends beyond the
exclusive privacy of the couple. Perhaps too their donation of
their property to the Republic goes further than Ralph's and
Indiana's occasional redemption of a few slaves. But there is
scant sense of real solidarity with the masses; theirs is an ideal
way of life set up as a model, not a practical programme for
change. It is a dream, a fantasy, not real life, parallel with and

opposed to the Gothic nightmare of the beginning, and its effectiveness as a message to others thereby somewhat limited. The moral implications of the tale as a whole also require scrutiny. Bozon-Scalzitti points out (pp. 5-7) that the values of civilization as opposed to nature are not unambiguously preferred. The fires of instinct are never fully extinguished and are not always necessarily wrong. In Paris, a reversal of values takes place whereby the physical Bernard's healthy vitality and curiosity represent life and energy, and to be over-civilised is to be dead. And perhaps Edmée's abundant fertility at the end is an essential part of Paradise, though the long years of their marriage are passed over so quickly that it seems as if she dies immediately after the wedding. The physical and the instinctive are usually either suppressed or criminalised by Sand, as in the rare enigmatic references to Edmée's hidden conflict, but they are still there—in Edmée's passionate declaration of love at the trial, or Bernard's sudden bursts of irritability with his servants. Although the main thrust of the narrative is towards an increasing spiritualization, away from the fatality of instinct, nature cannot be completely ignored.

Perhaps it is Arthur who comes closest to achieving the perfect balance. He remains for a year with the little group of the elect before returning to his country to pursue his study of the flora and fauna of the new world. Although full of compassion and high moral principles, his first love is for the natural world beneath his feet. As his fellow soldiers listen for the approach of the enemy, 'il était absorbé dans l'analyse d'une plante ou d'un insecte' (244). The great and the small, the ideal and the real, the abstract and the concrete are not necessarily as mutually exclusive as the conclusion of the novel might suggest; though she shows a preference for the ideal, Sand remains fully aware of the importance of the real and the physical as a fundamental part of all morality. Thus the message of the novel is relativised. It is contained not only in its conclusion but in the sum of its parts, in Bernard's physical vitality and Edmée's passion, as well as in the Utopianism of its ending.

Afterword

After 1837, Sand's life entered a more settled phase. In 1836, she had won her separation suit against her husband, and her affair with Michel de Bourges was coming to an end. She had first met Chopin in November of that year and in 1838 they began a relationship which was to last for nearly ten years, during which they regularly spent their summers together in Nohant and their winters in Paris. The author's life acquired a domestic, ordered quality which provided the essential frame for more than a decade of enriched literary activity, for in the 1840s and early 1850s, Sand's professional career as a writer reached its peak and she produced her most ambitious and notable work.

Perhaps the most impressive of these committed novels of the 1840s is the long narrative *Consuelo* (1842), which along with its sequel *La Comtesse de Rudolstadt* (1844) describes the life of another, similarly androgynous and exceptional *alter ego* of Sand. Consuelo is a talented young Venetian singer who travels widely in eighteenth-century Europe, is falsely arrested for conspiracy and imprisoned under Frederick of Prussia, marries the visionary Albert, comte de Rudolstadt, and finally joins his esoteric brotherhood of the 'Invisibles'. The work covers a wide range of historical figures and locations, Venice, Berlin, Vienna, and a huge number of issues—musical and artistic, social, political and religious. But with all its diffuseness, it tells a compelling story which goes far beyond the personal development of Consuelo herself. It has elements of the historical novel and a mystical allegory at the end, of the *Bildungsroman* and Gothic fiction. The themes of *Indiana* and *Mauprat* reappear—female desire and suffering, an Utopian belief in progress—, but are greatly enriched by the wider context and by the study of the dilemma of the woman artist, which was that of both the author of the novel and its heroine.

We find a similar combination of the personal, the historical and the moral in Sand's lengthy autobiography, *Histoire de ma vie*, which she began in 1847 and took a leisurely seven years to complete. The central figure is no longer an *alter ego* like Indiana, Edmée or Consuelo, but Sand herself who finally speaks in her own voice while still insisting that her story is that of every man (like Bernard) or every woman (like Indiana).

Yet she encounters the same difficulty as in her earlier texts of reconciling her own exceptional nature and experiences with the moral aim of this autobiography, which is apparently to console and enlighten through the narrative of her own sufferings which are also the reader's (whose gender remains ambiguous). So, as in *Consuelo*, the former oppositions remain, between the typical and the exceptional, male and female, public and personal, but as in *Mauprat*, though on a much larger scale, they enrich rather than obscure the main narrative thread.

There is little doubt that Sand could never have written these ambitious works had she not learned her trade in the earlier fictions of the 1830s, which treat the same preoccupations in a less elaborate and sophisticated way. She simply became more confident, more eloquent and more expert at infusing the traditional genres with which her readers were familiar with her own vision, in particular by putting a woman rather than a man squarely at the centre of the narrative. *Indiana* and *Mauprat* give us a vital access to the complex and changing person of their author, as both woman and writer, but they may also encourage us to penetrate further into her imaginative world as it receives its most complete expression in *Consuelo* and *Histoire de ma vie*, these two masterworks written a decade later.

Bibliography

Bozon-Scalzitti, Yvette. '*Mauprat* ou la Belle et la Bête, *Nineteenth-Century French Studies*, X, 1 (1981), 1-16.

Crecelius, Kathryn. *Family Romances. George Sand's Early Novels.* Bloomington: Indiana University Press, 1987.

Dayan, Peter. *Lautréamont et Sand.* Amsterdam / Atlanta, GA: Rodopi, 'Faux Titre', 1997 [1].

Dayan, Peter. 'Who is the Narrator in *Indiana*?'. *French Studies*, LII, 2 (April 1998), 152-61 [2].

Godwin-Jones, Robert. *Romantic Vision: The Novels of George Sand.* Birmingham, AL: Summa Publications, 1995.

Haig, Stirling. 'The Circular Room of George Sand's *Indiana*', in *The Madame Bovary Blues. The Pursuit of Illusion in Nineteenth-Century Fiction* (Baton Rouge & London: Louisiana State University Press, 1987), pp. 29-42.

Hecquet, Michèle. *Lecture du 'Mauprat' de Sand.* Presses Universitaires de Lille, 1990.

Hiddleston, Janet. *George Sand and Autobiography.* Oxford: Legenda, 1999.

Kadish, Doris Y. 'Representing Race in *Indiana*', *George Sand Studies*, XI, 1-2 (Spring 1992), 22-30.

Miller, Nancy K. 'Representing Writing: Ophelia drowns', in *Subject to Change: Reading Feminist Writing* (New York: Columbia University Press, 1988), pp. 84-90.

Naginski, Isabelle Hoog. *George Sand: Writing for her Life*. New Brunswick: Rutgers University Press, 1991.

Petrey, Sandy. 'George and Georgina Sand: realist gender in *Indiana*', in Michael Worton and Judith Still (eds.), *Textuality and Sexuality. Reading Theories and Practices* (Manchester University Press, 1993), pp. 133-47.

Reid, Martine. 'Mauprat: mariage et modernité chez Sand', *Romantisme*, 76 (1992), 43-59.

Schor, Naomi. *George Sand and Idealism*. New York: Columbia University Press, 1993 [1].

Schor, Naomi. Introduction to *Indiana*, tr. Sylvia Raphael. Oxford University Press, 'World's Classics', 1994, pp. vii-xxii [2].

Thomson, Patricia. *George Sand and the Victorians: her Influence and Reputation in Nineteenth-Century England*. London: The Macmillan Press, 1977.

Vest, James M. 'Dreams and the Romance tradition in George Sand's *Indiana*', *French Forum*, 3 (1978), 35-47.

Wingård Vareille, Kristina. *Socialité, sexualité et les impasses de l'histoire: l'évolution de la thématique sandienne d''Indiana' (1832) à 'Mauprat' (1837)*. Uppsala: Almqvist & Wicksell, 'Acta Universitatis Upsaliensis', 1987.

Yalom, Marilyn. '*Dédoublement* in the Fiction of George Sand', in Natalie Datlof *et al*. (eds.), *George Sand Papers. Conference Proceedings* (New York: AMS Press, 1982), pp. 21-31.